ALLEN BREED SERIES

The Allen Breed Series examines horse and pony breeds from all over the world, using a broad interpretation of what a breed is: whether created by the environment where it originally developed, or by man for a particular purpose, selected for its useful characteristics, or for its appearance, such as colour. It includes all members of the horse family, and breeds with closed or protected stud books as well as breeds and types still developing.

Each book in the Allen Breed Series examines the history and development of the breed, its characteristics and use, and its current position in Britain, together with an overview of the breed in America and worldwide. More difficult issues are also tackled, such as particular problems associated with the breed, and such controversies as the effect of the show ring on working breeds. The breed societies and their role in modern breeding policies are discussed.

BOOKS IN THE SERIES

The Appaloosa
The Arabian Horse
The Coloured Horse and Pony
The Fell Pony
The Hackney
The Hanoverian
The Irish Draught Horse
The Morgan Horse
The Mule
The Quarter Horse
The Trakehner
The Welsh Mountain Pony

The Hackney

The Hackney horse, indisputably the finest harness breed in the world. (*Photo: Bob Langrish*)

ALLEN BREED SERIES

The Hackney

Clive Richardson

J. A. Allen

London

British Library Cataloguing in Publication Data
A catalogue record for this book is available from the British Library

ISBN 0-85131-613-1

Published in Great Britain in 1995 by
J. A. Allen & Company Limited
1 Lower Grosvenor Place
London SW1W 0EL

Series editor Elizabeth O'Beirne-Ranelagh
Book production Bill Ireson
Printed in Great Britain by The Bath Press, Avon ·

Contents

Front cover: Holypark What's Wanted, champion Hackney harness horse at the South of England Show, 1984. (*Photo: Stuart Newsham*)
Endpapers: Mares and foals at Hart Hill Stud, Dorset. (*Photo: Annie Dent*)

Acknowledgements

The author would like to thank the following people and institutions for their help and assistance: Miss Susan Bailey; Dr Sue Baker, *Going Native* magazine; Mr Roger Bass; Mr William Binns; Miss Elizabeth Colquhoun; Dr Wynne Davies; Ms Annie Dent; Mr Neville Dent; Mrs Christine Dick; Grantham Library; Miss Susan Green, Librarian, Carriage Museum of America; Hackney Horse Society; Mr Martin Haller; Mr Edward Hart; Mr Richard James, *Carriage Driving* magazine; Miss Katie Maddocks; Mrs Fiona Manisty; Mr Jim Moor; National Sporting Library, Virginia; Miss Sally Oliver; and Mr Tom Ryder.

The author and publishers would also like to thank the following people and institutions for providing photographs and the permission to publish them: Ms Annie Dent; Mr Ken Ettridge; Mr Bob Langrish; Grantham Library; Mr Martin Haller; Mrs Fiona Manisty; Mr Jim Moor; Stuart Newsham; and Mrs C. Sharpe.

1 Introduction

The Hackney horse holds a unique position among the horse breeds of the world. Although essentially English in origin and character, having evolved to meet the demands created by social change in the period up to and following the passing of the Enclosures Act in 1801, the Hackney is now recognisable all over the world. As Sir Walter Gilbey wrote in 1898: 'In the Hackney, we have shape, action, courage, manners, staying power, and soundness. What would you more?' At one time its influence and fame matched, if not exceeded, that of the English Thoroughbred both in Europe and further afield.

The breed originated in the late seventeenth and early eighteenth centuries from the Norfolk Roadster and Yorkshire Trotter, two not dissimilar types of all-round utility horse which developed separately but simultaneously in two of the country's principal horse-breeding areas. Strong and active with legendary stamina and the ability to trot long distances at great speed, these early progenitors of the Hackney were essentially riding horses with the low, ground-covering stride peculiar to that class of horse.

Records dating from the last century and before provide ample evidence of the trotting feats of such famous horses as Nonpareil, who was driven 100 miles in nine hours, fifty-six minutes, fifty-seven seconds, or the celebrated mare, Phenomenon, who trotted seventeen miles in fifty-six minutes in 1800. Newspapers from that time abound with reports of trotting matches, many for private wagers, and successful roadsters earned great fame among the general public who loved a fast trotter.

But Hackneys were also all-round utility animals and would be expected to carry the farmer, and probably his wife too as a pillion, when he went to market or church or about his daily business, as well as occasionally providing a day's sport with the local hunt, and even taking a turn in the fields drawing a plough if the need arose.

When the development of a basic network of roads permitted the introduction of the mail-coach system a little over 200 years ago, Hackneys were employed in large numbers to horse the coaches. Even after the coming of the railways saw the demise of coaching, Hackneys were still the favoured breed for both private and commercial harness work on account of their stamina, speed and style.

The fame of the English Hackney was not restricted to these shores only, however, and since the early 1800s large numbers of horses had been exported to parts of the world as diverse as Russia, India and Argentina to improve and upgrade the

1

Nonpareil, famous trotting horse, competing in one of his timed road trials. (*Photo: F. Manisty*)

indigenous stock. So much so, that the House of Lords at one time formed a select committee to review the export trade in horses, which numbered 34,536 in 1897, many of them Hackneys or Hackney crosses. As well as contributing substantially to the breeding of cavalry, artillery, coaching, farm, and even pack horses at home and abroad, the Hackney has played a major role in the development of numerous pure breeds, including the American Standardbred, the Dutch Gelderlander, the Anglo-Norman or Selle Français, the Welsh Cob and the Australian pony.

It is quite probable that the Hackney would have suffered the same fate as the long-gone Yorkshire Coach Horse and Devon Pack Horse had the fashion for showing harness horses and especially high steppers not come into vogue at the end of the nineteenth century. The Hackney was ideally suited to this new sporting craze and, in the space of a few decades, underwent a sort of metamorphosis as the old roadster type, outdated by the whim of fashion and the advent of the motor car, was gradually replaced by the high-stepping show horse we know today as the modern Hackney. In the hands of wealthy breeders and the new class of professional trainers and exhibitors who flourished in the heady pre-war heyday of the show harness horse, the Hackney developed into a unique and distinctive breed. Within a relatively short period of time, it had changed from a general purpose riding animal to a specialist harness type with extravagant action not well suited to saddle work.

It was as a direct result of the growing interest in the breeding of fine harness horses that in the 1870s the Hackney pony was developed. It only took as many decades as its horse counterpart had taken centuries to get established, but quickly found a lasting popularity with the showing fraternity.

The decline of horse power, especially on the roads, the new age of the motor car, the depression of the 1920s and 1930s, the war years, and the closure of many of the big showing stables all contributed to difficult years for the Hackney. Indeed it seems incongruous that a breed developed specifically for harness work should survive beyond the horse-drawn era, but survive it did to enjoy new prosperity when riding and driving were rediscovered by the more affluent post-war generation as recreational pursuits.

Today the Hackney is well established, with breed societies in a number of different countries and a large international following of enthusiasts. It has disproved its critics by demonstrating its ability to compete equally with other breeds in modern harness sports like driving trials, and by showing that it does have a future outside

Outside the showring, many Hackneys are used for pleasure driving and non-competitive rallies. (*Photo: Clive Richardson*)

Part-bred Hackney mare, Hart Hill Lady Mildred, competing in horse trials. (*Photo: Annie Dent*)

the showring. Its potential as a crossing sire for the production of performance horses for eventing, show-jumping and other equestrian disciplines offers considerable scope, and there is every reason to believe that as the demands of today's equestrian market change the Hackney will also adapt, as it has done so often in its history, to fulfil that demand and claim its place as one of the breeds of the future.

2 Early origins of the Hackney horse

When John Marshall wrote his book, *The Rural Economy of Norfolk* (1787), he commented on the farm horses of Norfolk which 'stood hard work and hard keep in a remarkable manner'. They were not big horses, and they lacked the bone and substance of the heavy draught breeds of surrounding areas, but they were active workers and remarkable trotters, being 'well-fitted both for the saddle and draught' according to John Lawrence, whose *Philosophical and Practical Treatise on Horses* (1796) singled them out for particular mention. The horses of Norfolk, like those of Lincolnshire and Yorkshire, the other notable horse-breeding regions of the country, had been improved and developed through selective breeding over a considerable period of time to meet the new demands for horsepower brought about by social change and agricultural reform. The long and gradual process which took the small and wiry indigenous ponies of the region and transformed them into the farm horses described by Marshall and Lawrence, from which the modern Hackney ultimately evolved, began in Roman times, when the first known equestrian imports to Britain were made and the first steps taken to upgrade the local stock.

Ponies are not truly indigenous to Britain. As long ago as 1500 B.C. they either migrated or were driven across the channel by the nomadic hunters of the continent. By the time the Romans, with the expansion of their Empire, landed on these shores around 55 B.C., the descendants of the wild European pony were distributed throughout the British Isles, but they did little to impress the invaders, and Roman chroniclers including Julius Caesar wrote disparagingly of the ponies used by the ancient Britons for packwork or driving in lightweight chariots. They were small, twelve to thirteen hands at the most, and the Romans criticised them for their lack of size and substance which limited their usefulness as draught or riding animals.

During the initial years of the Roman occupation of Britain, repeated attacks by the ancient Britons, or Brigantes, made it difficult for the invaders to establish their position. It became apparent that if they were to maintain military supremacy and keep the hostile Britons at bay additional manpower resources were needed. A policy was implemented, which had previously been used with success in other parts of the Empire, of employing foreign mercenaries on a contract basis, and there is evidence of foreign units from many parts of the Empire including Scythia, Hungary, Gaul and, significantly, Friesland stationed throughout Roman Britain. Although this system survived up until the Roman withdrawal from Britain in the fourth century A.D., by that time these auxiliary soldiers had been replaced by Federates, a new type of mercenary not as closely integrated into the Roman military system. The Federates were more like small private armies under the command of their own chiefs who, at the end of each campaigning season, were handed a lump sum by the Army paymaster and were responsible for dividing it among their men as they saw fit. Unlike their predecessors, the Federates had to provide their own equipment, weapons and horses, and there is evidence from this period of Friesian Federates importing horses into this country.

Throughout Roman times, Friesland was an important province. Its fertile, sandy lowlands, now divided between the Netherlands and Germany, were one of the best horse-breeding areas in Europe and home to the Friesian horse, a breed of great antiquity which was well known to the Romans. The fourth-century Roman writer Vegetius spoke highly of these powerful black horses, which stood up to fifteen hands in height. This was large in comparison to other breeds of the day, although his contemporary, Tacitus, whose observations on horseflesh were usually fairly critical, described them as 'slow, heavy and powerful'. Aside from their strength and docile temperament which made them tractable and easy to handle, the Friesian horses were excellent trotters, with a good length of stride and the slight knee action which is still a characteristic of the breed. The Romans classified horses according to the purposes they were used for, and they recognised two distinct types of riding horse: those that trotted they called *Itinerarii*, and those which had been taught to amble they called *Ambulaturarii*. As stirrups were as yet unknown to the Romans, a horse which ambled was far more comfortable to ride, but a trotting horse was believed to have greater power and endurance and, at that time, it was certainly faster. The Friesian horses, like their Norfolk and Lincolnshire descendants, were trotters and as such the forerunners of the 'greate trottynge horse' of later times. The prepotency of the Friesian when crossed with other breeds or types meant that its influence was considerable, for not only did it pass on its strength, substance and equable temperament, but most of its descendants also inherited its black coloration.

The present-day Friesian horse is unlikely to be much different from its predecessor of Roman times, often referred to as the Flemish or Flanders horse, as up until the Middle Ages the breeds were virtually indistinguishable. The modern Flemish horse is now a larger and coarser type altogether as a result of breeding programmes to produce a heavier stamp of animal at the time when 'great horses' were needed as cavalry mounts for the armoured knights of Europe.

During the time of the Roman Empire, the Friesian people were great seafarers and traders, and their deep-bodied and broad merchant ships were capable of carrying

Friesian horse, one of the early ancestors of the Hackney, as it looks today. (*Photo: C. Sharpe*)

cargo both larger and heavier than most other sea-going vessels of that time. As well as their extensive trading activities, they were quite amenable to hiring out their craft for transporting personnel, equipment and even horses, and it is quite probable that they played a major role in the Roman invasion of Britain by ferrying the Roman army and later its mercenaries across the channel. Friesian horses owned by Federates in the employ of the Roman army must have been imported in this way.

The Friesian traders who came in the wake of the Roman invaders soon established themselves in Britain, as evidenced by place names like Friston in Lincolnshire, and there was a Friesian trading post in York where apart from cloth, metalwork and swords the stock in trade included horses.

When those mercenaries who owned horses returned home at the end of their contract period, many of their Friesian horses must have been sold off and left behind, especially in the vicinity of the east coast ports from which they sailed. These, together with horses imported and sold by enterprising traders, would be mainly stallions, as mares were not generally ridden or worked and the practice of gelding was still in its infancy. Bred on to the local native ponies, they produced a definite stamp of black or dark-coloured pony standing a little over thirteen hands but with plenty of

7

substance. In time this would become the Fen pony of Lincolnshire and an important foundation stone in the evolution of the Hackney. In the centuries following the Roman invasion of Britain, the Fen pony was bred in increasing numbers not only in Lincolnshire but in surrounding areas too.

From Norman times the selective breeding of horses began in earnest. At the Battle of Hastings in 1066 knights mounted on continental-bred cavalry horses of what would now be called light draught type dominated the scene as they would do on every battlefield throughout Europe for years to come, and the breeding of 'great horses' became a matter of national importance. It was believed that military strength would depend on heavily armoured knights mounted on such horses, and the business of acquiring foundation stock for the formation of studs necessitated looking again at the horses of Europe. As the breeding of war horses was a crown monopoly, it fell upon the ruling monarchs to initiate royal studs and breeding programmes. William the Conqueror imported into Britain horses of the 'Flanders breed', which was by this time one of the esteemed breeds of Europe on account of its relative size and weight – essential qualities in heavy cavalry horses. King John continued the trend by importing 100 'chosen stallions of the Flanders breed, and thus mainly contributed to prepare our noble species of draught-horses' (Miles, *Modern Practical Farriery*). Edward II also brought Flemish horses into the country as part of a policy to produce Britain's own breed of 'great horse', eventually to be known as the Old English Black and upon which Henry VIII mounted his cavalry. By the end of the nineteenth century, when the breed had been developed for agricultural use and become much larger, the old name was dropped and it became known as the Shire.

Although the Flemish horse of this period was sufficiently distinct to be classed as a breed in its own right, the term 'Flemish' seems to have been used in a generic sense to include examples of other heavy continental breeds, including the Brabançon, a Belgian draught breed, representatives of which had been imported since the days of Richard the Lionheart. While these heavy continental breeds played a major role in developing the Norfolk farm horse from the fast-trotting native Fen pony, they were too heavy and cumbersome to have retained much trotting ability themselves, and it is more likely to have been from later re-introductions of Friesian blood that the Norfolk horses inherited their action. Thomas Blundeville, who was born and lived in Norfolk, in his book, *The Foure Chiefest Offices of Horsemanship* (1558), alludes to the popularity of Friesian horses in Britain when he makes little mention of British breeds but does speak of 'a Friseland', and nearly forty years later Bishop Joseph Hall in his satirical verses writes of the merchant who 'hires a Friezeland trotter, halfe yard deep, to drag his tumbrell through the staring Cheape'.

Further evidence is provided by yet another writer, Nicholas Morgan, who listed the horse and pony breeds in order of popular esteem in England in his book, *Perfection of Horsemanship* (1609), and put the Flanders horse and Friesian in tenth and thirteenth place respectively and ahead of any British breeds.

By the early nineteenth century the Norfolk farm horse was as well established as the Lincolnshire Fen pony was scarce. A writer of the time commented that a great many ponies 'used to be reared in Lincolnshire in the neighbourhood of Boston, but the breed has been neglected for some years, and the closure of the fens will render it extinct'. The drainage of the fens also had another effect on the local horse population, for it is highly probable that the Dutch drainage and land reclamation experts who came to supervise the operation brought black trotting horses with them. Encouraged by William, Prince of Orange, trotting had become a popular sport in the Low Countries, and it was soon to be taken up with enthusiasm in Britain in the form of ridden matches and timed road races. The 'excellent variety of well-shaped black nags' described by John Lawrence in his *History and Delineation of the Horse* (1809) as 'sometimes excellent trotters' and 'doubtless originating in Flemish stock', suggests a link with these later imports.

Although horses which ambled were popular in England for certain ridden purposes up until the early 1700s, the tradition was to employ trotting horses for any function that demanded staying power and speed. Nowhere was this more strongly felt than in Norfolk and Lincolnshire, where references to the use of trotting horses can be traced back to the fifteenth century. Thomas Blundeville, writing of the farm horses of his native Norfolk 150 years later, summed it up accurately when he pointed out that brood mares should be 'of a high stature, strongly made, large and faire, and have a trotting pase . . . for it is not meet for divers respects that horses for service should amble'. A gradual increase in wheeled traffic on the roads towards the latter part of the seventeenth century brought a demand for strong trotting horses capable of pulling the heavy and badly designed vehicles along the muddy, pot-holed and rutted roads. When, in response to public demand, improvements were made to the roads and it became possible to travel longer distances with greater speed, a need arose for faster trotters. Ambling horses which had neither the traction power for heavy work nor the speed for fast road travel quickly went out of fashion. At the same time increased mobility of the population had resulted in a steady market for saddle horses. The old Norfolk breed, described in the *Farmers Magazine* in 1802 as 'among the best working horses in the island', were as good under saddle as they were in a plough, having replaced oxen which were slower for most types of farm work. Samuel Dyball's mare, Smart, was probably typical of the Norfolk horses of

9

her day when in 1767 she was described as being 'very famous for hunting, ploughing and travelling the road'. According to S. Sidney in his *Book of the Horse:*

> They were strong, for they had to carry, besides the horseman in heavy jack boots, leather breeches and broad-skirted coat, a heavy horseman's cloak, saddle-bags, and holsters for a pair of pistols. They were tolerably swift, for a rider might owe his safety to his nag's pace. They had good shoulders and plenty before the pommel, capital legs and feet.

They were also the penultimate ancestor of the modern Hackney.

The word 'nag', which is derived from the Anglo-Saxon 'hnegan' meaning to neigh, was the term used from early times for a riding horse. The Normans brought their own word, 'haquene', which had the same meaning, and the combination of the two, first latinised into 'hakeneius' then anglicised into 'hackney', resulted in a word in common use from the twelfth century and used to describe any type of saddle horse. As early as 1303, Robert Mannyne, a monk from Bourne in Lincolnshire, wrote of 'Ilk on his hakneye', and in *Piers Plowman*, written by Langland circa 1350, mention is made that 'Ac hackeneyes hadde thei none, bote hackeneyes to hyre', while Chaucer, who lived in Norfolk for a time, spelled the word 'hackeney' and 'hacknay'. The word was also sometimes used to describe horses for hire, and Samuel Johnson's dictionary defines a hackney as a hired horse, although the Reverend Samuel Pegge, a Norfolk antiquarian writing in 1807, believed it implied 'a common horse for all purposes of riding, whether for private use or for hire'. Whether in its original form or abbreviated to 'hack', the word was soon accepted as meaning *for hire*, and even the London prostitutes were known as hackney wenches in the 1730s. Since 1634 when the first hackney stand, predecessor of the modern taxi rank, was established in London, the public coaches which plied for hire had been known as hackney coaches and their drivers as hackney-men or hackmen. So numerous did they become that during the reign of Charles II hackney coaches were banned from standing in the streets waiting for custom as they caused traffic jams, and they were ordered to remain in their yards until summoned. However, as Samuel Pepys noted in his diary in November 1669: 'Notwithstanding that this was the first day of the King's proclamation against hackney coaches coming into the streets to stand for hire, yet I got one to carry me home.' London had around 2,500 of these vehicles on its streets at this time and the sad state of the over-worked and weary horses brought into popular use the term 'hackneyed' to mean 'worn out by common use like a hired horse'. Soon anything trite or common-place was thus described, and the prefix 'hack' was applied to people of little skill in certain occupations like journalism, where bad reporters are still sometimes labelled as hack-writers by Fleet Street. Hack is now taken to mean a general riding horse, the definition ascribed to hackney in times past. As the use of the word hackney referred originally to a class of horse rather than a specific breed or type, in much the same way as the word cob is used today, it was always spelt with a small 'h'.

There is evidence to suggest that the demise of ambling horses in favour of trotting horses which occurred as a result of the improvement in roads and the changing use of hackneys brought about a gradual re-defining of the name. Samuel Johnson also described a hackney as a pacing horse, and the current definition of the old word *haquenée* in modern English dictionaries is 'an ambling nag' and in modern French 'an ambling saddle mare'. However, by the nineteenth century the name hackney clearly meant a trotting horse or one specifically for use on the road. As William Taplin in his *Sporting Dictionary* (1805) writes: 'It is the peculiar province of the Hackney in England to carry his master 12–15 miles an hour to cover where the hunter is in waiting, and sometimes to carry back the groom with greater expedition.' The word 'trotter' had also been in use since the 1400s to differentiate between horses which trotted and those which ambled, both often still being described as hackneys, but the word 'roadster' which came into common use in the early nineteenth century specifically meant a fast trotting horse.

'The Horse Dealer', engraving by George Walker, shows two roadsters being led to the town.

The Norfolk Roadster and his Yorkshire-bred contemporary were linked by their common ancestry on the distaff side of Flemish and Friesian blood, which gave them many similarities in type and size. Alexander Morton, in an address to the Glasgow Agricultural Discussion Society in 1891 in which he compared the Norfolk and Yorkshire types of Hackney, said that the former was 'a much heavier horse, longer in the barrel, rounder in the shoulders which, however, are as a rule better laid back. He is also plainer about the head but has generally more action, particularly behind.' He attributed the regional differences to more of 'the old British blood in the Norfolk Hackney'. The Chapman horse, a general utility agricultural and pack type which stood a little over fourteen hands and which eventually helped found the Cleveland Bay, also had influence on the Yorkshire Trotter, while the Yorkshire Pack Horse, according to the agricultural writer Vero Shaw, was widely used by Hackney breeders of the period, for the pack horse was 'most unquestionably a valuable breed and hence regret must be expressed that it was ever permitted to become extinct'. However, as Charles Rogers pointed out years later in an essay reviewing the origins of breeds and sent to the Royal Agricultural Society, 'there can be no doubt that the so-called roadsters, nags and cobs were more or less admixtures of breeds'.

It was not until the demand for a better class of road horse, as a result of increased road travel and the success of the mail-coach system, encouraged the introduction and availability to mare owners of high-class stallions, that the Norfolk and Yorkshire horses achieved any degree of individual uniformity. Up until then local availability was the main criteria in selecting a breeding stallion, and the inevitable element of in-breeding which this system dictates meant many regional sub-types existed. Often a successful and prepotent stallion would found his own local dynasty in a particular area, and it was not until farmers and horse breeders recognised the existence of a lucrative and growing market for better quality horses that they became less parochial in their outlook and more selective in their choice of stallions. This coincided with the advertising and availability of quality stallions which were 'travelled' during the breeding season in a chosen locality, where they would cover mares for an agreed stud fee. An example was the prominent Thoroughbred stallion, Jalap, of whom more later, whose stud fee was five guineas for blood horses and two guineas for Chapman mares. The tradition of travelling stallions was born out of necessity, for in rural areas farmers might have to lead, ride or drive their mare to wherever the stallion was kept in order to get her covered, and this could be very time-consuming, especially at a busy time in the farming year. If the mare had a foal at foot such a journey may not have been possible at all, and this further encouraged the use of the nearest available stallion irrespective of its suitability.

Under the travelling system, which was introduced soon after the turn of the eighteenth century, the stallion's owner or groom led the stallion on a planned weekly circuit, stopping at those farms where the stallion's services were required. The same circuit was repeated weekly throughout the travelling season, which traditionally began on the second Monday in May and finished on August Bank Holiday Monday. The stallion man was responsible for finding accommodation for himself and his horse in the district they travelled, often staying overnight at the farms they visited during the week and then returning to a lodging house for the weekend before setting off on the Monday morning to travel their route again. In areas containing many breeding mares, several stallions might be travelled by their owners, thereby giving mare owners some degree of choice while compelling stallion owners to travel animals of quality if they were to be successful in securing custom. Although advertisements for travelling stallions were placed in the local newspapers, members of the farming community – who owned the largest percentage of breeding mares – were not great readers, and they were more likely to be convinced by the sight of a fit and well-turned-out stallion in the flesh than the written word. The long distances travelled each week by the stallions and their handlers soon brought to light any hint of unsoundness or lack of stamina, so that only the fittest horses lasted the season, and the whole system was self-regulating as good stock-getters were in demand and those which produced inferior stock were not.

From the middle of the eighteenth century, newspapers began to carry advertisements for stallions at stud, including one for 'a famous stallion, an Arabian, by the size fifteen hands three inches, and strength proportioned' which appeared in the *Norfolk Mercury* on 12 April 1741. There had been earlier imports of both Arab and Barb horses, as since Elizabethan times the sons of wealthy families had been encouraged to travel abroad for the forerunner of what would become the Grand Tour of Europe. Many brought back Arab or Barbary horses which could be purchased at reasonable cost on the dockside of ports like Marseilles, and the horses were ridden home, which said much for these north African imports in view of the road conditions and the distances involved. There is a record of a bay Barbary mare in the possession of the owner of Whitby Manor in 1621, although it is probable that she was locally bred by a Barb stallion as few Barb or Arab mares were imported at this time. When the breeding of racehorses began to escalate into something of a science, the number of Arab imports increased dramatically, and many found their way into Yorkshire and the eastern counties. It was recorded that between 1803 and 1814 eighty-four Arabians, forty-seven Barbs, thirty-two Turks and four Persian horses were imported into England. 'Where but from the Eastern horse', wrote A. J. Cassatt in an article on the Hackney published in 1892, 'could he get the broad forehead, the lofty carriage and high croup, the brisk cheerful temper, the extreme docility combined with the resolute courage that alike mark the true Hackney and the Arabian horse.'

Lady Wentworth, an authority on Arabian horses, believed that the Andalusian horse of Spain had also played a role in the development of the Hackney, which is quite probable for after the death of Elizabeth I in 1603, her successor James I worked to forge stronger links with Spain. He was rewarded with among other things the gift of a considerable number of fine Andalusian horses bred at the Royal Stud at Cordoba. These horses became the responsibility of the Master of the Horse, the Duke of Buckingham, a royal favourite, who acquired the vast Helmsley estate in Yorkshire through his prudent marriage to Lady Katherine Manners in 1620. He took most of the Andalusian horses up into Yorkshire where they were crossed with local stock and ultimately absorbed into what would become the Cleveland Bay and Yorkshire Trotter.

Other stud advertisements of the early eighteenth century were for stallions of other breeds and types including Norfolk Cobs, which must have been similar or even the same as the Norfolk farm horses mentioned earlier, hunters, road horses and Chapmans. A notice of 1741 advertised a stallion which was claimed to have 'the strength of a troop horse with the beauty, shape and speed of a running horse', while other announcements placed more emphasis on performance, and trotting in particular, by giving details of distances covered, weights carried, and speeds achieved. A typical example was Smiling Ball, a chestnut horse, advertised in 1746 to 'trot 14 miles an hour with ease'.

It was, however, the Thoroughbred which was to have the greatest influence in upgrading the progeny of the local farm and pack-horse mares into the famed road horses eventually to be known as Hackneys. William Taplin, writing in his *Sporting Dictionary* of 1803, said: 'In tracing back the respective blood of the Thoroughbred and Hackney, it was found that after 150 or 200 years they became so much akin on one side of the breed that it was impossible to separate them.' Most of the Thoroughbred stallions being travelled at stud in the eastern counties at this time still showed much of the character of their Arab, Barb or Eastern ancestors, and a great many of the stallions in use throughout Yorkshire, Lincolnshire and Norfolk were direct descendants of the three foundation sires of the Thoroughbred, namely the Godolphin Arabian, the Byerley Turk and, most particularly, the Darley Arabian.

Some of the many Thoroughbred stallions used during the development years of the Hackney were either celebrated trotters themselves or they became famous because their progeny were fast road horses. One or two of these early blood horses were of special importance, including Jalap, a stallion whose pedigree could be traced back to the Oxford Arabian, and whose successful racing career came to an abrupt end when he broke down at a race meeting at York in the late 1760s. His influence on the breeding of quality horses was recognised by William Marshall who, in his book *The Rural Economy of Yorkshire* (1788), commented that the improvement in local horses over the preceding two decades 'was principally effected by one horse, Jalap, a full bred horse whose pedigree and performance are well known upon the turf'. His son's name, Trotting Jalap, speaks for itself. Another notable Yorkshire-based Thoroughbred stallion was President, whose son, Bay President, won a class for the 'best stallion for hunters' at Northallerton in 1840, and fifteen years later at the age of twenty-two won a class at Malton for the best roadster stallion.

Among the many notable non-Thoroughbred stallions in use at the time a few predominated, and none more so than the legendary horse described by John Lawrence in *The History and Delineation of the Horse* (1809). 'The best trotters which have appeared', he wrote 'and which are now to be found in Lincolnshire, Norfolk and their vicinity, have proceeded from Old Shields.' Phonetically written and frequently misspelt, the horse's name was more often written as Shales or Schales, and in his later years he was sometimes referred to as Old Shales or the Original Shales. As it was customary to refer to horses according to who owned them, it is probable that Shales was the name of the horse's owner, a theory supported by the known existence of both the names Shales and Shields in the Norfolk area. Shales was evidently a most influential horse, as all Hackneys are ultimately descended from him. He was foaled around 1755 and he was by the Thoroughbred, Blaze, a son of the Duke of Devonshire's racehorse, Flying Childers, who despite his lack of stature distinguished himself on the racecourse before going on to make a name for himself at stud. Shales' dam was described as being a 'strong common-bred mare', probably a farm or cart horse. Flying Childers' sire was the Darley Arabian, named after Thomas Darley who purchased him in Aleppo in 1704 and who, in a letter written to his father the same year, said the horse's real name was Manaka. William Scawen Blunt believed this was not actually the name of the horse but a crude translation of the Arabic word *muniqi*, which referred to a particular strain of Arab noted for their speed and much used for racing.

Through Flying Childers, the Darley Arabian was responsible for many of the best road horses of the period. Henry F. Euren, the first historian of the Hackney breed as well as the first secretary of the Hackney Horse Society, commenting on stallions standing at stud in the mid nineteenth century, mentions several horses by either Flying Childers or his son, Blaze, but it was the Shales strain that was to carry the Darley Arabian's name into posterity. Records from the time are sketchy and often contradictory or confusing, which makes it difficult to ascertain facts with any guarantee of accuracy, but, as the names of popular horses were widely copied and there were over eighty stallions called Shales in the first volume of the stud book published in 1889, the impact of this horse on the early Hackneys must have been phenomenal.

Old Shales' most famous son, Scot Shales, produced two influential sons himself, the first being Marshall's Hue and Cry. He was named after 'the hue and cry he raised while dashing along the road . . . he was a horse of rare temper and courage, a true trotter, and got good stock'. The other son, Thistleton Shales, had a long and successful career at stud, living to the age of thirty-four years when he died as a result of an accident which broke his back, but his real fame was as the sire of Marshland Shales, the most renowned of the Shales family. Described in an issue of *The Sporting Magazine* as being 'acknowledged both the speediest and stoutest trotter of the time', Marshland Shales achieved fame throughout the eastern counties of England with his performance in trotting matches in which he was never beaten. His most famous match, against Richard West's horse, Driver, was reported upon in the 6 August 1810 issue of the *Norwich Mercury*. It described in detail the running of the £200 wager in which the famous horse trotted seventeen miles in fifty-eight minutes, carrying twelve stone. Marshland Shales was not a big horse, as he stood barely fifteen hands, but he was reputedly well built with plenty of bone. It is remarkable that

Marshland Shales. An early-nineteenth-century engraving from the original painting by Suffolk artist E. Cooper of Beccles. (*Photo: F. Manisty*)

YOUNG
GREY SHALES,

The Property of James Mell,

WILL COVER THIS SEASON,
1841,

AT CROWLE AND IN THE NEIGHBOURHOOD,

At One Guinea and a Crown each Mare.

YOUNG GREY SHALES was got by Old **Grey Shales**, his dam by Sir Andrew, grandam by Quetlavaca, his great grandam by Old Weazle.

Old Grey Shales was got by Chadd's Champion **Shales**, his dam, a superior grey mare, by Old Pretender, whose sire was Jenkinson's Old Fireaway, which trotted **two** miles in five minute, and was afterwards Sold for **1000** guineas.

Chadd's Champion Shales was got by Marshland **Shales**, which horse trotted seventeen miles in one hour, carrying fourteen stone, beating the noted horse Driver, for two hundred guineas, and afterwards stood Champion of England.

Young Grey Shales is descended from the first **blood** and the fastest trotters in the kingdom; he is six **years** old, a very sure foal-getter, stands fifteen hands **three** inches high, and for action and breeding, as a Nag, he stands unrivalled; his dam, grandam, and great grandam were all masters of seventeen miles within the hour.

☞ *The money to be paid the last Round.*

J. PEARSON, PRINTER, EPWORTH.

such an outstanding animal should have been sold as a yearling in 1803 for the sum of only twelve guineas.

Another famous grandson of Flying Childers was a Thoroughbred stallion called Joseph Andrews, owned by two gentlemen from Beverley in Yorkshire, who had also owned Blaze at one time. Whilst in their ownership, Joseph Andrews had been sent to stand at stud in Lincolnshire for a time and, as a result of this, Thomas Jenkinson of Long Sutton in the fens came to own a mare by him. As a breeder of Hackneys Jenkinson was already well known, having bred Marshland Shales' sire, Thistleton Shales. This Joseph Andrews mare, when covered by Driver, a son of the Original Shales, produced a colt which they called Pretender, although the name was later changed to Fireaway, probably because of the former's political associations. Among the famous descendants of Jenkinson's Fireaway was West's Fireaway, credited with being 'the fastest trotter in the kingdom' according to an advertisement of 1822, and who was out of a noted trotting mare who herself was by a Thoroughbred. West's Fireaway's two most famous sons were both out of mares which were virtually Thoroughbred. One of them was by the Derby winner, Skyscraper, and her colt, Burgess' Fireaway, stood at stud at a livery stable in Piccadilly, London, for five years before returning north, this time to Yorkshire. The other son, a bright bay named Silver-Tailed Fireaway, was out of a grand-daughter of Regulus.

Burgess' Fireaway was the sire of another famous foundation stone of the Hackney breed, The Norfolk Cob, which according to an article in *The Sunday Times* in 1839 was 'out of a Shields mare, and reputed to be the fastest trotter that ever stepped'. Such accolades were not reservedly given, for The Norfolk Phenomenon, a 15.2 hand red roan son of The Norfolk Cob, was, according to *The Sporting Magazine*, 'allowed by all competent judges to be one of the best and fastest trotters ever shown'. The Norfolk Cob ended his days in the West Indies where he was shipped at the age of nearly twenty by his owner, Sir William Codrington, who had an estate there.

It is interesting that although many of these early Hackneys carried a high percentage of racing blood in their veins, some being nearly pure Thoroughbred, others were nearer to the old farm-horse type. John Lawrence, writing of the fame of the Original Shales in Lincolnshire in the 1770s, adds: 'He was either rivalled or succeeded by Jenkinson's Useful Cub, a horse of very different breed.' Useful Cub, whose name was probably a misspelling of cob, was reported as being 'got by a black cart horse . . . out of a Chapman's mare', although he was still able to trot 'above the rate of twenty miles an hour, though he carried seventeen stone'.

Another influential horse bred by Thomas Jenkinson was Young Pretender, who was by Jenkinson's Fireaway out of a mare by Joseph Andrews, possibly even the same mare which was the dam of Fireaway. Sold to Christopher Wroot of Long Sutton and thereafter known as Wroot's Pretender, the horse distinguished himself both as a breeding sire, earning £760 stud fees in three seasons, and as a trotter. Wroot himself claimed of the horse that 'when five years old he trotted 16 miles in one hour . . . for which he received 200 guineas, and which is the greatest performance ever done by any horse of the same age'. His achievements as a breeding stallion included siring a horse called Steven's Bellfounder whose son, Jary's Bellfounder, was exported to America in 1822 where he helped to found the American Standardbred.

In later years these American trotters became so popular that in 1864 a representative of the breed called Shepherd F. Knapp was brought over to England where he was to have a significant influence on the Hackney. The Shepherd, as he was popularly known, was a chestnut horse with a blaze, foaled in 1857 and bred by George Snell of Turner, Maine. His sire, The Eaton Horse, also a chestnut, was in-bred to Messenger, the English-bred Thoroughbred shipped to America in 1788 where he became the most important foundation sire of the American Trotting horse. The Eaton Horse was described by H. C. Merwin in *Road, Track and Stable* as 'a long-striding lumbering beast', and the same author wrote that The Shepherd's dam was 'a stout little Morgan mare and an exceptionally high stepper'. She was by Whalebone (also known as The Clark Horse) whose sire, Sherman Morgan, was felt by many to be the most influential son of the original Justin Morgan as he sired a prominent line through Black Hawk and his son, Ethan Allen, sire of over seventy winners of trotting races. The Shepherd was himself raced for several seasons in America with some success, and he was listed in Hiram Woodruff's *Trotting Horse of America* where it was noted that he trotted the mile in 2 minutes 41 seconds. In England he won several prestigious trotting matches, and in 1865 was taken to France where he remained for over a year, winning a two-and-a-half mile trotting match in the Bois du Boulogne and siring some notable horses which in turn had some influence on the Anglo-Norman breed. The following year and back in England, The Shepherd gave an exhibition of his trotting ability at the London Horse Show, and a report in the *Illustrated London News* of 2 June 1866 read:

> Shepherd F. Knapp, the property of Mr J. Edwards of Ealing, quite carried out his great fame when McCormack, his constant guide and counsellor, drove him to a match cart, and the assembly fairly 'rose at him' as he rattled along up the side stretch . . . He is a very wiry looking, bald-faced chestnut, not more than 15.2 hands, as the terms of the prize indicate, with rather a dish face, lightish back ribs and legs, which have seen, as Punch's dealer observes, a deal of ' 'ammer, 'ammer, along them roads'.

The Shepherd's much publicised appearance at the London Horse Show was followed by many similar exhibitions at shows around the country over the next few years. At an exhibition at Aintree in 1868, he greatly impressed Major Stapylton of Myton Hall, Helperby in Yorkshire who was looking for a suitable stallion to improve the action of the local Yorkshire Trotters. He bought The Shepherd for £500 and showed him at the Great Yorkshire Show at Beverley that year, where he won the roadster stallion class, beating Ambition, winner at the Royal Show that year, and the famous Yorkshire-bred horse, Denmark. Samuel Sidney, who witnessed his win, wrote in his *Book of the Horse* that The Shepherd had 'action as beautiful as anything ever seen in this country . . . for pace no English roadster could touch him'. Lumley Hodgson, a respected equestrian authority of his day, writing in the 1882 journal of the Royal Agricultural Society said: 'The horse set his mark on all his produce, and Young Shepherds have been sought after, and have commanded long prices. His extraordinary action will long be remembered; he had the merit, uncommon in American trotters, of possessing all-round trotting action.' The Shepherd's stock were much sought after, his owner selling a two year old to the French Government for £250 and a yearling for £90, high prices at that time. One of his daughters, a bay mare called Primrose, bred by Aquila Kirby of Market Weighton, became one of the top brood mares at William Burdett-Coutt's Brookfield Stud. Primrose was out of a Yorkshire-bred mare called Nelly, who was by the great roadster stallion, Achilles, out of a Thoroughbred mare called Sall who was given to Aquila Kirby's father, Robert, by J. J. Broadley of Scarborough who bought her at York as a thirteen year old for 235 guineas. Primrose, foaled in 1875, was a big winner in-hand in the showring, including first at the Royal Show as a two year old, and one of her descendants was the famous Hackney stallion, Buckley Courage. Other progeny of The Shepherd included Goldfinder and Washington, the latter breeding many great high-stepping show horses including the piebald mare, Movement. The Shepherd lived to be twenty-four years of age when, due to ill health, he was put down in September 1881.

Also in Market Weighton in Yorkshire was Robert Ramsdale, the man responsible for bringing some of the best Norfolk horses up into Yorkshire to improve the local Hackneys. He owned Ramsdale's Performer, a son of Wroot's Pretender, and The Norfolk Phenomenon, who was said to have 'wonderful action'. The Ramsdales, Robert and his son Philip, owned and bred many outstanding horses, one of their most famous being Ramsdale's Wildfire, which was by Burgess' Fireaway out of a mare reputedly by Marshland Shales. Another of their horses was Ramsdale's Fireaway, a bay horse standing 15.2 hands, whose illustrious pedigree included such great names as Burgess' Fireaway, his sire, and on his dam's mainly Thoroughbred side, the ex-racehorse Jalap. The bloodline was continued on through stallions like Ramsdale's Phenomenon, Taylor's Performer, Lund's Merrylegs, Scott's Fireaway, and the excellent strain of Hackneys bred by the Cook family whose farm in the Yorkshire Wolds became the premier breeding stud in the north, a position it held for over a century.

It is significant that the names of influential horses are repeated time and time again in Hackney pedigrees, for the breed is based on family lines emanating from

Jackey, a son of Marshland Shales, who in 1852 trotted five miles in 14 minutes, 5 seconds, carrying ten stone. (*Photo: F. Manisty*)

outstanding stallions. These delineations of the breed were often obscured by the lack of written records and the fact that the oral tradition, through which details of famous horses were passed, was prone to exaggeration, misinterpretation and more than a measure of deceit. Stallion owners in the early years of the breed were not above fabricating the pedigree of their horse and claiming it came from a more popular bloodline in order to attract business. This was especially true when it might involve considerable financial gain, and more than one stallion owner made his fortune from a successful horse. The practice of using common names like Fireaway or Wildfire also makes it difficult now to differentiate with certainty between horses of the same name, and this problem is compounded by the different names an individual horse may have been given as he changed hands during his lifetime. It was not until stud book records for the Hackney began to be kept towards the end of the nineteenth century that more accurate information could be made available to breeders.

Similarly, the accounts of trotting matches are open to conjecture. The reputation of the early Hackneys was centred on their trotting speeds, along with the distances they covered and the weights they carried. Some of the first accounts of trotting wagers and timed road trials which appeared in the *Norwich Mercury, Yorkshire Gazette* and other publications seem quite incredible by modern standards. In 1794 *The Sporting Magazine* carried a report of a mare who trotted forty miles in three hours carrying eighteen stone, and such stories were not unusual. There are records even of a donkey trotting sixteen miles in an hour pulling two men in a barrow. Although some of these outstanding feats may have been exaggerated, most were probably true, for the makers of wagers which carried a substantial cash prize would have made sure that both the distance and the speed were correctly recorded to avoid disputes or disagreements. Moreover, the early Hackneys were required to possess no other qualities than speed and stamina, which made them singularly suited to such races. It is interesting to note that the ages of successful horses were usually recorded too, many of the match winners being quite old horses like Cartwright, a thirty-year-old gelding which trotted thirty-two miles in two hours on the road between Stilton and Cambridge. As John Lawrence pointed out, however: 'It is remarkable that trotters, unlike gallopers, do not lose their speed from old age, many having been known to trot as fast at 20, or even near 30 years of age, as they did in their prime.'

The coming of the railways and the end of the coaching era led many breeders to believe that the day of the harness horse was over and that the Hackney's heyday had passed. Coinciding as it did with the agricultural depression of 1835–45, many farmers gave up horse-breeding altogether and sold their stock off, totally unaware that instead of facing extinction the Hackney was about to experience a revival the impact of which would be felt around the world.

3 The Hackney Horse Society and the early shows

In 1873 Henry F. Euren, editor of the *Norwich Mercury*, turned his attention from cattle breeding to the trotting horses of Norfolk and Lincolnshire, the performances of which in trotting matches had often been reported in the pages of his newspaper. The export trade for Hackney stallions had grown steadily over the preceding twenty years, and at home the increasing demand for Hackneys for both private and trade use had more than bridged the gap created when commercial coaching ceased, depriving breeders temporarily of a regular market for their horses. Despite the coming of the railways, Britain's industrial expansion together with the prosperity of the towns and cities saw an increase in private vehicles from 60,000 in 1841 to 500,000 by 1900 in England alone. If trade and public vehicles were included in the figures, the numbers could be tripled. Bearing in mind that the Hackney was the most popular driving horse of the time and therefore a breed of significant importance, Euren felt it imperative to research and record the history of the breed, including its blood

Mrs Angela Taylor driving her Hackney horse, Appleton Bonny Lad, to a milk float in a trade turnout class, still popular in the 1980s. (*Photo: Jim Moor*)

lines, and to this end he set out, in his own words, on the 'self-imposed pleasurable task of preparing the remedy by gathering the materials for a stud book'. He travelled extensively throughout the eastern counties talking to breeders and enthusiasts, and the initial products of his research were set down in an article entitled 'Renowned Norfolk Trotting Horses' which appeared in the *Livestock Journal* of 25 June 1875. Not only did Euren discover to his surprise that he was the first to study the breed in any depth, but the interest generated by his article convinced him of the need for a Hackney breed society.

On 30 June 1878, Euren organised a meeting of interested parties at Downham Market in Norfolk, where it was agreed to establish a breed register for Hackney horses. At that time the breed was also known by other names, including Norfolk Roadster and Yorkshire Trotter, but the name Hackney was chosen because it was non-geographical and avoided the intense rivalry that existed between breeders in the two counties. It was also the name in most common use at the time. Over the next five years Henry Euren worked assiduously until, as he wrote, his 'researches were sufficiently advanced to allow of my announcing the issue of such a register'. This he did in 1883, when volume I of the Hackney Stud Book was published at his own expense. The interest with which it was received can be gauged by the fact that it was briefly reviewed in *The Times* newspaper. On 30 June of that year, following a public meeting held in Norfolk and chaired by Anthony Hamond, the Hackney Stud Book Society was formed, with Euren as secretary, assisted by his son Frank, and a council consisting of thirty members, most of whom were farmers and breeders. The Prince of Wales, later to be Edward VII, agreed to be patron. The annual subscription rate was set at one guinea, and the registered office of the Society was at the editorial offices of the *Norwich Mercury*, although there was also a branch office in Chandos Street, London.

Six months after the Society was formed it had attracted 300 members, and there was no problem getting breeders of Hackney types, including Norfolk Roadsters and Yorkshire Trotters, to register their stock as horse-breeding was then very lucrative and the possession of registration documents and a known pedigree could only enhance the value of an animal. There was no inspection of type prior to registration in those days and breeders merely wrote what they knew of the horse's parentage on the form of application for registration which they then signed as true and correct. Not surprisingly, there were inevitable anomalies among the registrations in the early stud books, including a 13.3 hand Arab stallion entered in volume XIII, and from the start Hackneys with one Thoroughbred parent were openly accepted for registration. In 1888 the registration rules were amended to include American trotting stallions recorded in the American Trotting Register but used within the United Kingdom, and the same year the council at its meeting on the Royal Show ground at Nottingham voted to inspect for registration 'mares whose pedigree cannot be determined and which are presented for examination as suitable for breeding Hackneys'. Mare owners had to write to the secretary giving all known details of the mare, and enclosing the inspection fee and a veterinary certificate verifying the age and soundness of the horse. Stallions were not eligible for inspection. When M.P., a stallion whose dam was inspected, won the stallion championship at both the 1892 and 1893 Hackney Shows it caused a storm of protest, as breeders claimed that a horse with a parent of unknown breeding should not have won, and consequently the eligibility rules for registration were revised and tightened up.

In 1891 the Society changed its name to the Hackney Horse Society as it felt its aims now extended far beyond the publication of breed records. The new Society literature announced that its objectives were:

1. To promote and encourage the breeding of Hackneys, roadsters, cobs and ponies.
2. To compile and publish stud books, to offer facilities for the sale of pedigree Hackneys and to issue recognised transfer and export certificates.
3. To hold shows and obtain for tenant farmers and breeders the use of sound stud horses of the best stamp.
4. To offer prizes for Hackneys and ponies at the shows of various agricultural societies, etc.

In the early years of the Society there was some internal controversy over what constituted the correct type of Hackney. Foreign buyers who purchased large numbers of horses preferred a larger, more coachy type of animal. It is clear that breeders had tried to meet their requirements for there is evidence of well over fifty stallions foaled prior to 1850 all standing 16 hands or more. William Burdett-Coutts, a founder member of the Society and the Member of Parliament for Westminster, was adamant that no Hackney should exceed 15.3 hands in height, and the Royal Agricultural Society restricted the Hackney classes at its shows to animals not exceeding 15.2 hands, although the Hackney Society was later instrumental in getting this rule rescinded. Others favoured a smaller animal still and were quick to point out that many of the famous foundation horses of the breed like Marshland Shales were little more than fifteen hands. Eventually a height of 15–15.2 hands was accepted as average for the breed, although by 1901 most of the forty stallions entered at the London Show were well over 15.3 hands. The inclusion of 'ponies and cobs' in the revised objectives of the Society alluded to the obvious confusion that existed as to whether ponies could be deemed Hackneys or not. With no agreed directive on the subject, Hackneys of any size were accepted for registration and it was to be some years before the pony question was resolved satisfactorily.

The question of correct type was even more difficult to rationalise, for as Vero Shaw pointed out:

> it is a remarkable thing that no official standard of excellence has been laid down . . . were there some such pronouncement in existence with respect to the Hackney, matters would be made far easier for breeders, and the public would not be indulged by the spectacle of some remarkable decisions in the show ring.

In 1891, Alexander Morton, a council member and Hackney breeder from Ayrshire, drew up a standard of excellence for the Hackney which was generally accepted as the breed standard of the day. In his view the ideal Hackney was a 'short legged powerful little horse, standing 15–15.2 hands high', with a head that was not over small and set on a neck of medium length, as he believed that a long neck gave a blood or coaching impression. Deep and well laid back shoulders were essential as, in his opinion, 'short straight shoulders are good for nothing, and must be avoided at all hazards', and he advocated a short back with the ribs well sprung from the back-bone, and well-developed muscles along each side forming a hollow along the spine. The hindquarters had to be broad and strong with the thighs well let down to the hocks. He believed that there should be a gentle droop to the quarters as this gave 'a much more graceful outline, besides giving more leverage to the muscles of the thighs'. Short powerful legs, large hocks and knees with plenty of muscle above and 'as much bone below as can possibly be got', large fetlock joints, not overlong pasterns, and feet of medium size and rather deep in the hoof were all essential. 'Large feet often denote low breeding, and cannot stand long journeys', he advised, and the hair and skin 'should not be over fine as the animal is not so tough if this quality is developed too much'.

Evidently Morton's breed standard described a utility animal foremost but one which was adapting into a more stylish carriage horse eminently suited to the showring for, after pointing out the importance of straight action, he adds: 'the higher the action all round, he will always be sure to fetch the more money'. To the coaching proprietors, farmers and dealers of earlier decades, lofty action was wasteful and undesirable, but to the new generation of more affluent owners and showring exhibitors, it was essential. 'Quiet and affectionate in his stable', Morton

Mr G. Dudley's supreme champion stallion, Wentworth Kestrel, shown by Craig Purver. Lofty action, once considered wasteful and undesirable, is now an essential characteristic of the modern Hackney. (*Photo: Jim Moor*)

concluded, 'there is yet in his composition that something which, at the merest word or touch, can electrify him into the liveliest and brightest of animals.'

Although Alexander Morton dismissed the subject of colour with the statement that provided the animal conformed to the breed standard any colour was acceptable, other Hackney enthusiasts felt the matter warranted a stronger directive. Because bay or dark brown were the most favoured colours for carriage work, the proliferance of chestnut Hackneys concerned many enthusiasts, as they feared the Hackney might become an exclusively chestnut breed like the Suffolk Punch. Vero Shaw, commenting on the disdain with which fashionable society viewed chestnut horses for harness work, emphasised that 'the Hackney is placed at a distinct disadvantage when opposed to the Oldenburgs, Holsteins and other varieties of foreign horses, which are all sizeable and fine movers, whilst the prevailing colours amongst them are sound bays and browns'. Despite the commercial disadvantages, chestnut Hackneys were to out-number other colours for some years to come, and at the 1907 Hackney Show

220 of the 302 horses entered were chestnuts. Roan Hackneys, many tracing back to The Norfolk Phenomenon, a red roan stallion foaled in 1825, were becoming scarce, and greys, despite their popularity in the early years of the nineteenth century, were even rarer. Browns were more common, but black Hackneys, once favoured for troop horses, were in decline, although as W. J. Gordon wrote in 1893: 'at one time the black horses of the Household Cavalry came almost entirely from Yorkshire and North Lincolnshire, most of them being expressly bred for the purpose'. Piebalds and skewbalds, once not uncommon, were also being ousted by the ubiquitous chestnuts, although those that remained were generally regarded highly. The last strain of coloured Hackneys was bred at Cole Ambrose's Stuntney Stud at Ely in Cambridgeshire in the early decades of this century, and many were exported to an Argentinian customer called Enrique Gath who owned a department store in Buenos Aires and used the distinctively marked horses for drawing the store's delivery vehicles. Gath was also a keen coaching man and drove a four-in-hand of piebald Hackneys on coaching drives which often lasted several days. A *tropilla* of spare horses, many bred by Gath from imported stock, followed behind the coach.

Abundant white markings were frowned upon in horses destined for formal carriage work as they were regarded as flashy and ostentatious, and Vero Shaw wrote disapprovingly of 'the practice of many judges to be very tolerant of white splashes

Mr Billy Ryan driving Buckland Perfectionist. Abundant white markings are not uncommon in some bloodlines. (*Photo: Jim Moor*)

on the belly, white faces and lips'. Ironically, the stallion responsible for so many of the chestnut Hackneys also threw a large percentage of foals with too much white for the prestigious carriage trade, but his overall influence on the breed earned him a position of some importance in the history of the Hackney. Denmark was a 15.2 hand chestnut bred by William Ricknell of Yorkshire in 1862. A grandson of Taylor's Performer, Denmark was successfully shown both by his breeder and by George Bourdass, who later bought the horse, but it was as a breeding stallion that he made his reputation, consistently producing quality foals with size and substance. As Denmark was 'travelled' for over twenty years in the East Riding of Yorkshire and his stud fee never exceeded three guineas, he had ample opportunity to leave his mark on the horses of the region. The most famous of his many progeny was a chestnut stallion with four white socks called Danegelt, for which Sir Walter Gilbey paid 5,000 guineas in 1892 to prevent him being sold abroad. Danegelt himself bred many champions including Rosador, a chestnut with four white legs and a blaze, and it is interesting that many present-day Hackneys with abundant white markings trace their lineage to this bloodline.

Other notable stallions whose influence helped mould the Hackney at this time included Triffit's Fireaway, foaled in Yorkshire in 1859, and a descendant of The Norfolk Phenomenon; D'Oyley's Confidence, a brown stallion also carrying the blood of The Norfolk Phenomenon and who was to play an important role in the pedigrees of Hackney ponies as well as horses; Wreghitt's Wildfire, a bay roan horse who was eventually sold to go to America; and Lord Derby II, another brown horse and one whose blood, like that of D'Oyley's Confidence, would run in the veins of many famous Hackney ponies.

It was the exhibiting of Hackneys in the showring as much as anything else that initiated the gradual transformation of the breed into the specialist show horse that we know today. When trotting races began to lose their popularity in the second half of the nineteenth century, many agricultural societies, whose aims were to improve the standard of farm livestock bred in their districts, began incorporating more classes for Hackneys and roadsters in their schedules and prize lists. Most towns and districts held an annual show of some description, the classes generally being restricted to breeding or youngstock. Shows like Bridlington, Howden, Market Weighton, Driffield and Pocklington were all established venues in the show calendar of early Hackney exhibitors. As the eligibility rules for Hackney classes at these shows were not clearly defined, a variety of types ranging from heavy cobs to blood horses might be shown, and judges often merely selected those animals whose type they preferred irrespective of the individual merits of the exhibits. When the demand from abroad for Hackney stallions of heavier type declined and the first motor cars appeared on the roads, progressively minded Hackney breeders were quick to realise that the future lay in breeding for the showring, and stallions which produced that type of progeny soon became fashionable.

Two of the most eminent sires for the showring were Polonius and Matthias, half-brothers out of a wonderful mare called Ophelia, believed by many to be a near perfect example of a Hackney. Ophelia, who was by either Denmark or Danegelt (no one seems quite sure as her dam was covered by both) was foaled in 1884 and purchased by Lord Londesborough the following year for his stud near Market Weighton. Although she inevitably enjoyed considerable success in the showring, it was as a brood mare that she is best remembered. Her progeny included both notable harness horses and successful breeding stallions. Shortly before the Earl's death in 1898, his stud was dispersed by public auction and Ophelia was sold for 525 guineas, while her four-year-old son, Polonius, who was by Wreghitt's Wildfire, made the record price of the day when he was purchased by William Burdett-Coutts for 575 guineas. Burdett-Coutts was American by birth and christened William Logan Ashmead Bartlett, but he came to England and was put through Oxford and later employed as private secretary by Baroness Angela Burdett-Coutts, a spinster thirty years his senior, whose vast fortune was connected with the Coutts bank. She caused a scandal in London Society when she married her employee during an Adriatic cruise in 1881, and soon afterwards he changed his name from Bartlett to Burdett-Coutts. She used her considerable influence to launch him on a successful political career while he used her enormous wealth to set up one of the most important studs of the pre-war years. Polonius became a leading stallion at Burdett-Coutts' Brookfield Stud, which up until its closure in 1912 produced many of the top harness horses of the day, and when Robert Whitworth purchased Polonius in 1902 he had to pay £2,000 for the privilege.

Ophelia's other famous son, Matthias, a three-year-old grandson of Lord Derby II, was also sold at the Londesborough sale and was purchased by William Scott of Carluke in Scotland. During the years that followed he excelled as a sire of harness horses and became even more successful than his celebrated half-brother. Other progeny of Ophelia put up for auction at the Londesborough sale included Sir Augustus, a stallion believed by many to be superior to his half-brother, Matthias. He got little opportunity to demonstrate his worth as his buyer, Sidney Carnley, a Lincolnshire lawyer, sold him to the eccentric Lord Ashworth who shipped him out to his stud farm in County Galway and he was not heard of again. The stud was closed down by the government in 1941. Philador, a young stallion by Rosador, and

Dennis Midgley driving Mr R. Cowan's Heathfield George, Wembley champion, 1979–80–81. Organisers of the first Hackney Show in 1885 could never have envisaged the continued success of the breed nearly a century later. (*Photo: Jim Moor*)

Fortinbras, a gelding by Wreghitt's Wildfire and therefore full brother to Polonius, comprised Ophelia's other progeny. Fortinbras, under his new name of Heathfield Squire, was the most successful show harness horse of his day and he was eventually exported to America by his new owner, 'Judge' W. H. Moore, a wealthy exhibitor.

In 1885 the then-named Hackney Stud Book Society held its first modest show at the Agricultural Hall, Islington, London. Despite fears that neither exhibitors nor the general public would support the show it was a resounding success, as evidenced by a report in *The Times* of 5 March 1885, which announced: 'the first show of the Hackney Stud Book Society closed last evening . . . everything went off very well which is all the more gratifying seeing that the Society was only formed

31

about eighteen months ago'. The schedule was restricted to nine classes, six for stallions and three for mares, attracting an excellent entry of 132 horses and ponies, 94 of which were stallions. In order to avoid accusations of bias from rival exhibitors in Yorkshire and Norfolk, it was agreed to select one judge from each area along with a third judge from elsewhere. At the first show, J. F. Crowther from Yorkshire, J. Morton from Norfolk, and Lord Combermere from Shropshire officiated, and they found their champion stallion in the ten-year-old brown Norfolk-bred horse, Reality, who was by D'Oyley's Confidence. Reserve champion was the smaller Lord Derby II, then thirteen years old, and perhaps significantly of Yorkshire breeding. The champion mare was Henry Moore's Princess, a daughter of Denmark, the stallion whose progeny were to dominate the Society's second show in 1886 when they won five of the eleven classes as well as both the stallion and mare championships. By 1895 total entries for the annual show had risen to 383, and by 1911 they had increased to 626 as the show Hackney enjoyed wider popularity.

The London Hackney Show, as it was popularly known, received considerable

Miss Sylvia Brocklebank driving her grey Hackney, Optimistic, winner of the open harness class at Grantham Show in 1913. (*Photo: Grantham Library*)

attention from the press in 1891 because, as a result of the Prince of Wales becoming president of the Society, several members of the royal family were among the spectators, including Queen Victoria, who had honoured the Society by becoming patron, and the Empress Frederick. The membership by this time had increased to nearly 1,200.

Six years later classes for Hackneys in harness and under saddle were added to the schedule, producing forty-one entries in the five driving classes and an amazing thirty-eight entries in the riding class, which virtually filled the small ring at the Agricultural Hall. Although the performance classes were dropped the following year in order to make room for stallion produce classes, they were reinstated again in 1899, when the winner of the twenty-five strong under 15.2 hands driving class was a dun gelding called Norbury Squire, who was sired by Denmark out of a Norwegian Fjord pony mare. At the time, horses by a Hackney stallion out of part-bred, cross-bred or even pony mares were acceptable for some classes. An innovation at the 1900 Hackney Show was a class for ponies in harness, but it only produced twelve entries which was disappointing in comparison to the in-hand stallion classes which often sported forty or fifty entries. However, the other pony classes were sufficiently well supported to be grouped together as a separate section rather than scattered through the horse classes.

As the show harness horse reached its heyday in the early years of the twentieth century, the London Hackney Show was joined by a number of other prestigious shows staging classes for Hackneys, including the Richmond Horse Show and the International Horse Show, first held at Olympia in London in 1907. The farmers and tradesmen who had been the backbone of the showing fraternity in the early years were being replaced by wealthy 'fanciers', as they were called, and many employed the services of professional trainers to prepare and exhibit their Hackneys. One such owner was C. E. Galbraith of Dumfries in Scotland, whose early successes were largely attributable to the skill of his stud manager, Thomas Black, who won the junior mare championship and the reserve senior championship at the 1896 London Hackney Show with two of Galbraith's Hackneys. Thomas Black had five sons, all of whom became successful Hackney trainers in both Britain and America as well as the forerunners of public show stable proprietors, and they remained at the forefront of the Hackney showing world for the rest of their days. Other trainers tried to emulate them but few were as successful. Robert Black's daughter, now Mrs Cynthia Haydon, went on to become the greatest Hackney whip of her day, and also the owner, with her husband Frank, of the most successful Hackney stud of recent years.

The popularity of Hackneys with tradesmen, especially butchers, fishmongers and bakers who all liked a flashy fast-trotting horse for delivery work, had originally discouraged members of fashionable society from getting involved with the breed, as they felt Hackneys smacked of 'trade'. By the time the Hackney Horse Society enjoyed royal patronage and breeders included some of the leading society figures of the day, the old prejudices had been lifted and the Society flourished as the value of good Hackneys soared. William Scott's Thornholme Stud in Lanarkshire where Matthias stood at stud held annual sales, and in 1906 ten of Matthias' youngstock averaged £319 each, an excellent price in those days. Other breeders were being similarly rewarded.

The generous prize money offered at the Hackney shows was enhanced in 1912 by the awarding of harness medals which, by permission of H.M. King George V, bore a portrait of His Majesty who, it was reported, took a keen interest in the affairs of the Society and became patron for a period.

The outbreak of war in 1914 thwarted the Society's ambitious plans to hold the

show the following year at Olympia with an extended schedule to include more harness classes. Instead, the show which had been held over three days was cut back to just two, and was held for the next three years in March at the Agricultural Hall. Entries were substantially reduced – only 195 entries in 1916 – and in 1918 and 1919 the show was curtailed to cater for stallions only and moved to Newmarket where it was thought to be safer. Many Hackneys had been commandeered for the war effort by the army remount officers, and their suitability as troop, draught or pack horses had not gone unnoticed. During 1914 horses with the Society's certified export papers had left these shores for Argentina, Brazil, Canada, the Cape Colony, Chile, France, Germany, Holland, Hungary, Italy, Japan, Natal, Orange Free State, Russia, Spain, Transvaal and the United States of America.

Unsure of how long the war might last but convinced that the army would need a steady supply of horses for some time to come, two new classes were included in the schedule for the Newmarket Show for 'stallions suitable for breeding artillery and

The Hackney became a favourite of late-eighteenth-century tradesmen, and this is reflected in the showring today. Grantham Dairy Co.'s prize-winning milk float (*opposite page*) drawn by a Hackney pony, circa 1900 (*Photo: Grantham Library*); Mr Billy Ryan (*below*) driving his Hackney horse, Birkhouse Ben, to a butcher's box cart in the 1980s. (*Photo: Jim Moor*)

army horses. To be judged on conformation, true and straight action.' The winner in 1918 was Findon Grey Shales, a ten-year-old owned by H.R.H. The Prince of Wales. The classes were discontinued after the 1927 show.

Despite the activities of the army remount officers who only requisitioned horses, not ponies, and whose compensatory payments were poor anyway, the prices of Hackneys suddenly fell drastically. At a public auction of forty registered Hackneys owned by Thomas Smith of the Shirley Hackney Stud on 20 September

Horses of the Shales strain:
Silver Shales (*top*), a well-known ride and drive animal. He was an excellent polo pony and once carried the Duke of Edinburgh to umpire a match. In 1978, at the age of thirty, he was driven in harness at the head of a parade of fourteen Shales horses before H. M. The Queen.
Findon Grey Shales (*centre*), foaled in 1908, also had royal connections, being sold to the then Prince of Wales (later Duke of Windsor). Royal Shales (*bottom*) was purchased in 1922 by Mrs J. C. Colquhoun from the Duchy of Cornwall estate.
(*Photo: F. Manisty*)

1916, yearling fillies made up to £31, two-year-old fillies £36, and a matched pair of geldings made £46 and £73 respectively. By comparison, a Brougham by Morgan of Long Acre, London, made only £11, a dogcart by the same maker £7. 10s. and a four-wheeled Mills buggy with two pairs of shafts, a pole and splinterbar only fetched £3. 10s.

In 1921 the Hackney Show was moved back to London but poor entries and a disappointing public attendance meant that it was not financially viable for it to remain at its old site, and the show was moved to Doncaster where the Corporation had generously offered the free use of a suitable venue. After several successful years at Doncaster, financial problems forced the Society to move again, but this time it formed a partnership arrangement with the Royal Counties Show which, like the Royal Show, moved to a different venue each year. The first combined show was held at Reading in 1930 where the great mare, Modern Maid, produced by Bob Black, made her memorable showring debut in the capable hands of brother Jimmy to win both the novice and open harness championships.

The inter-war depression years saw the demand for Hackneys slip even further as many of the private showing stables closed while motors took over on the roads. When Albert Marshall sold his Fairview Hackney Stud at Stranraer, the seventy horses including eleven mature stallions averaged less than £10 each, and those breeders who persevered did so with little hope of financial reward. In spite of these problems, the standard of horses being bred had not suffered and the famous and influential horses bred at this time included in their number such Hackney legends as Buckley Courage, four times champion at the Hackney Show; Nork Spotlight, winner of many harness championships – the rule debarring stallions from competing in harness classes having been lifted; and Nork Spotlight's most famous foal, Erlegh Maiden, reserve supreme champion at the 1935 Hackney Show when only a yearling. She was eventually purchased by Frank Haydon for his Hurstwood Stud where she proved herself to be an outstanding brood mare, as well as the most influential Hackney mare since the great Ophelia.

When war broke out again in 1939, the Hackney faced the most critical period in its long history and many breeders genuinely felt the breed was heading for extinction. Although petrol rationing brought a temporary revival of interest in driving, it did little to help the Hackney which was seen as a specialist show animal, and stock quickly became unsaleable. Furthermore, the local agricultural committees, whose remit was to ensure that all available land was used for food production, openly disapproved of the breeding of Hackneys which contributed nothing to the war effort, and some used their not inconsiderable powers to commandeer land for

Instead of facing extinction as prophesied, the breed enjoyed new prosperity in the post-war years and many new studs appeared, including W. A. Sully's Holypark Stud in Kent. Mr F. A. Neachell's Holypark What's Wanted, driven by Michael Neachell. (*Photo: Jim Moor*)

crops. Joseph Morton of Norfolk had his land requisitioned by the government authorities in 1940 as they felt the land occupied by his horses could be put to better use, and he reluctantly sold his horses off for pitifully low prices. Fortunately for the breed, Robert Black was able to buy several of the Hackneys including the stallion, Solitude, which he showed with great success in later years. However, at that time with the shows cancelled 'for the duration' and great uncertainty for the future, his purchases could easily have been a great waste of the few pounds he paid for them. The Society struggled on as best it could but at the 1941 annual meeting the president, Claude Goddard, gloomily predicted: 'I fear that there will be no Hackneys after the war unless special efforts are made now to maintain the breed.'

With the return to peace-time, the Hackney Horse Society took stock of the breed and, suitably encouraged, arranged for the first post-war show in the sale yard at Crewe in 1946. The modest one-day show comprising only in-hand classes was a far

Holypark Rantara, by Holypark What's Wanted, a prolific winner in the showring in the 1980s, driven by her owner Mr Jimmy Wenham. (*Photo: Jim Moor*)

cry from the fashionable three-day London shows of forty years earlier, but it was quite well supported by exhibitors and spectators, who watched the thirteen-year-old stallion, Solitude, take the championship. The show remained at Crewe until 1949, although the harness classes were revived and held at Salisbury at the Royal Counties Show in 1948. The policy of holding the in-hand and harness classes at different venues continued, with the in-hand classes moving to a venue at Derby where they stayed for four years while the harness classes continued to move annually from site to site with the Royal Counties Agricultural Society. In 1953 both sections of the Hackney Show were amalgamated with the Royal Counties Show which was ultimately incorporated into the South of England Agricultural Society's annual show held on the permanent show ground at Ardingly in Sussex, where the Hackney Show has remained ever since.

By 1948 the demand for Hackneys had recovered to such an extent that two of the

Hackney horse, Ingfield Black Prince, driven by Joe Quigg to a show wagon. Pneumatic-tyred vehicles including this and the viceroy are appropriate to Hackney driving classes. (*Photo: Jim Moor*)

stallions sold at the dispersal sale of the Oakwell Stud to make £400 and £600 respectively, although other lots were harder to sell, including a yearling filly which only got bid to £48 and an unbroken four-year-old gelding which went under the hammer at £39. Ten years later a reduction sale at the Haydon's Hurstwood Stud saw mares selling for £500, £580 and £680 as the breed's fortunes recovered and the revival of driving as a leisure activity brought harness horses renewed popularity, the British Driving Society having been formed the previous year.

Although the showring Hackney was immensely popular with the general spectating public, the surge of interest in horse driving afforded the Hackney new opportunities outside its more traditional role in the showring which it needed in order to widen its scope and progress further.

4 The Hackney Pony

Throughout the long history of the Hackney horse, there are occasional references to fast trotting ponies, giving the impression that the modern Hackney pony developed alongside its larger counterpart over many centuries. This was not the case.

Up until the eleventh century, the equine population of Britain consisted mainly of ponies, as the horse breeds which developed later were all the result of selective breeding for specific purposes, and selective breeding was virtually impossible under the Anglo-Saxon method of horse management. Prior to the setting up of the Royal parks, which were in effect large secure enclosures where selected animals were turned out for the purpose of breeding heavy cavalry or 'great horses', ponies had traditionally been kept on the rough marginal ground surrounding village settlements. They fared better on this land than other types of livestock, with the exception of goats, and they were certainly less vulnerable to the depredation of wolves, which survived in England up until the fourteenth century, than either sheep or cattle. The drawback to this method of husbandry was its lack of control over breeding policy. It meant that the pony stock of these early breeders never improved with the passing years, and in many cases it deteriorated due to indiscriminate in-breeding, the use of inferior stallions, and the inadequate care of youngstock.

When the selective breeding of horses was introduced, in all cases size was paramount. With war horses, the bigger and more substantial the animal the more effective it was on the battlefield. The pack horses bred at the abbeys and monastic houses in Yorkshire needed size too, as this increased their carrying capacity, and when the fertile soils of Lincolnshire were ploughed and cultivated large and heavy farm horses were developed specifically for this work. The early racehorses, or running horses as they were often called, were also sizeable animals and so it was inevitable that the early roadsters, in whose veins the blood of all these other breeds and types ran, would be horses and not ponies. The quality of the grazing in the eastern counties of England was also in the main good enough to maintain horses of larger size compared to many other areas of the country, and ponies were gradually ousted as the new horse breeds took over. Significantly, although there are nine native ponies in Britain, none are indigenous to the counties which gave rise to the Hackney.

During the reign of Henry VIII, royal decrees were passed with the aim of encouraging the breeding of larger horses, although other essential qualities like conformation and type were still left to chance. The king issued a series of laws intended to eradicate

41

ponies and produce in their stead animals suitable for military use, including one law which made the local magistrates of certain shires responsible for an annual gathering of all horses grazing on common ground within their locality. Any stallion below fifteen hands and any mare below thirteen hands had to be slaughtered, along with any foals deemed unlikely to make the necessary minimum height. Similarly it was made an offence to graze on common ground any colt 'above the age of two yeare and not being of the altitude and height of fifteen handfulls'. The reason given for these statutes was 'for the encrease of stronger horses' which would be 'a great help and defence to the realm and a great comoditie to the inhabitants thereof'. It was also decreed that every archbishop and duke was to keep seven trotting saddle-horses; every bishop, marquis or earl, five; and other people of rank between three and one according to their position. As these horses would most likely all be stallions, they would have needed to stand at least fifteen hands in height.

The trotting ponies of the eastern counties mentioned in later times were probably under-sized animals of Hackney horse parentage, although some breeders like John Atkinson, a flax spinner from near Harrogate in North Yorkshire, specifically bred ponies in preference to horses. In the early eighteenth century he produced a strain of trotting pony that was renowned throughout the region. His stock were all descended from a mare called William Deighton's Wonderful Girl, the previous owner's name being prefixed to the pony's according to the custom of the time. This mare was by the well-known Thoroughbred stallion, President, out of a mare brought down from Scotland and possibly of Galloway breeding. One of Wonderful Girl's many successful progeny was a pony called Jenny Lind, who was by Merry Driver, a Norfolk Roadster. She was owned by a gentleman called J. W. Scriven from Otley, who was once asked to umpire a trotting match near Harrogate between two sixteen-hand roadsters. He did so by riding a few yards behind the participants on his mare, who was then twenty years old. When one of the roadsters broke into a gallop, disqualifying itself, its rider beckoned Scriven to teach his gloating opponent a lesson, which he did by bursting through on his old pony to win the match. The strain must have died out after Atkinson's day for it is not heard of again and, despite occasional references to other pony-sized roadsters, the true Hackney pony was not to make its debut until towards the end of the following century. It had no direct link to these earlier trotting ponies.

It is said that while the Hackney horse took several centuries and a geographical area the size of the eastern counties to evolve as a breed, the Hackney pony was developed by one man on his private estate within the space of a few years. Christopher Wyndham Wilson of Rigmaden Park, near Kirkby Lonsdale in the old

Hackney pony mare, Eaglestone Jacintha, champion senior pony mare at the 1987 Hackney Horse Society show, with her day-old colt foal, Semley Sparrow, who in 1992 became supreme champion pony at the Hackney Horse Society show. (*Photo: Annie Dent*)

county of Westmorland, was a shrewd and enterprising man whose progressive ideas were far ahead of their time. He invented the silo for the storage of winter fodder, a revolutionary idea now universally adopted but at that time treated with scepticism by both the local farmers and the agricultural societies which Wilson addressed regularly. He was a pioneer of deer and fish farming, and trout reared at Rigmaden were put on the night train to London and eaten at the breakfast tables of the expensive London hotels a few hours later. He imported some of the first Friesian cattle into this country, and introduced Suffolk sheep into the north of England to try and improve the local flocks. Local people remember that he delighted in novelty, owning the first motor car in Westmorland – registration number EC1 – in which he regularly drove into Kirkby Lonsdale, the local market town, accompanied by one or more of his pet otters, a tame badger and a monkey. He installed electric power into Rigmaden in 1883, making it only the second country house in England to be lit by electric light, and although Rigmaden is now just a roofless shell the water turbines which once provided its power are still in perfect working order. Standing six feet tall with an imposing white beard, the former High Sheriff of Westmorland had a restless and enquiring mind which he applied to a variety of diverse interests with great success. When, in the 1870s, he became interested in breeding ponies he can have had little idea of the impact his experimental breeding was to have or that he was about to create the only non-native breed of pony in the country.

The term Hackney pony had been in common use for some time, but it seemed to be applied to a variety of pony types whether they included any Hackney blood or not. The confusion over what constituted a Hackney pony was evidently shared by the Society which, when formed in 1883, encompassed cobs and ponies as well as Hackneys and roadsters but without ever defining what the former really were. Ponies and horses were not separated in the stud books, and they were virtually judged by the same criteria in the showring, although there was at first no official breed standard laid down for Hackneys of any height. At the first two London Hackney shows there was a class for pony stallions and one for cob stallions, but the entries were so poor that the classes were deleted from the schedule for the third show, and the term 'cob' was never used again.

In 1890, Hackney pony classes for both stallions and mares were revived in response to the surge of interest created by new breeders like Christopher Wilson, and the champion mare on this occasion was the piebald, Magpie, by the great Hackney stallion, D'Oyley's Confidence, out of a 14.2 hand skewbald mare called Spot whose ancestry included both Thoroughbred and Arab forebears. Foaled in 1878, Magpie was a substantially built but quality pony standing under 14 hands. She won over 400 first prizes both in harness and under saddle during her illustrious career, including ten wins at the Royal Show, and she was often shown side-saddle in ladies' hack classes by her owner's daughter, Miss Pope, who described her as 'a most pleasant ride'. She was sufficiently well known for a full page to be devoted to listing her winnings in the second volume of the Hackney stud book, but as a brood

Mrs E. E. Vyse's Sunbeam Super Star, supreme champion Hackney pony, shown by Noddy Vyse, 1986. The distinctive pony character which distinguishes the Hackney pony from its larger counterpart is clearly evident. (*Photo: Jim Moor*)

mare she was a disappointment and it is likely that her progeny, including her foal by Danegelt which they named Magpie's Danegelt, grew beyond the permitted height for ponies.

There were also instances of ponies with no Hackney blood at all being shown as Hackneys, including Lord Zetland, a Shetland pony owned by the Marquis of Bristol, which won second prize in the class for Hackney stallions not exceeding 13.3 hands at the Society's 1886 show. This trend was unwittingly encouraged when at one time the London Hackney Show included a class for Hackney stallions not exceeding ten hands. However, the majority of animals shown as Hackney ponies were really small part-bred Hackneys and, as such, small horses rather than true ponies.

Christopher Wilson's aim was to produce a harness pony with quality, substance and stamina, extravagant action, tremendous presence and plenty of *pony* character.

He most specifically did not want to breed small horses like the so-called Hackney ponies being produced by other breeders. The difference lay in that elusive quality known as pony character, and Sir Gilbert Greenall, later Lord Daresbury, believed by many to be the greatest pony judge of his day, held that 'pony character is derivable from a pony cross more or less remote, and its possession makes the difference that exists between a true pony and what may be merely an undersized horse'. Vero Shaw, the agricultural reporter and a keen enthusiast of the Hackney, tried to define pony character more precisely when he wrote that it 'embodies facial expression, carriage, and character, with smallness of stature, and an indomitable spirit, which all true ponies possess to an extent quite out of proportion to the size of their bodies'. Christopher Wilson was very aware that he could only imbue this rare quality into his stock by breeding up from ponies rather than by breeding down from horses and, with this in mind, he began selectively buying small native pony mares to form the foundation stock for his stud.

His first purchases were Fell pony mares, a breed indigenous to the counties of Westmorland and Cumberland where they had existed as a relatively pure breed since post-Roman times. There are no details of these purchases as it was to be another twenty years before a section for Fell registrations was opened in the stud books of the Riding and Polo Pony Society, but it is likely that they would be smaller than present-day Fell ponies – perhaps around thirteen hands – and either brown or bay, the preference for black Fells coming later. In a letter to another pony enthusiast, Wilson said that the Fell pony in his part of the country was 'a cart horse in miniature', adding that it was 'used for all kinds of farm work'. According to Roy Charlton, writing in his book *A Lifetime with Ponies*, Wilson 'selected the very best purely-bred Fell pony mares then living in Westmorland and Cumberland', and an article published in *The Horse* in 1905 supported this and said that Wilson's strain 'had been founded on a long sustained cross of the Hackney and Fell pony'. Not all the foundation mares were Fells, however, and Wilson experimented with ponies of other breeds too, including Welsh. Hackney horse breeders had tried this cross themselves as Henry Euren, secretary of the Hackney Horse Society, revealed when he commented that:

the Welsh mare has in two generations given excellent results, when mated with sizeable stallions. The second generation has the staying power, the hardiness, and the vigour of the mountain pony; while, with due care of the youngstock, there has been sufficient growth, and 15.2 hh has been the height attained.

Wilson sought all the former qualities in his ponies though not the height, and he restricted the size of his ponies by the use of a small stallion, in-breeding over successive generations, and a rather Spartan regime for the care of his youngstock. There is also evidence of a 13.3 hand bay mare by a Thoroughbred among the foundation mares, and this pony, The Pet, who was bred by Daniel Miller of Worcester in 1869 and who had won a first prize at the Royal Show on at least two occasions, was to prove one of his best brood mares.

It was important to Wilson's aims that the stallion he chose to use on these foundation mares had outstanding presence and action, and he found an ideal candidate in Yorkshire which he subsequently bought and brought home to Rigmaden. Sir George was a brown stallion, standing just under fourteen hands, and bred by William Walker of Shadwell near Leeds in 1866. His sire, Sportsman, was a grandson of Taylor's Performer, and his long pedigree could be traced back to such famous names

Mr C. W. Wilson's pony stallion, Sir George, patriarch of the Hackney pony breed.

47

as Burgess' Fireaway, Old Shales, Joseph Andrews, Flying Childers and the Darley Arabian. Nothing is known of the breeding of Sir George's dam, Polly. Not only was Sir George 'an extraordinarily good-looking pony' as one writer described him, having won first prize at the Royal Show on eight successive occasions before Wilson bought him, but he was also a prepotent sire who passed on to his progeny his wonderful conformation, dazzling action and, not least, his great presence. Sir George became, in the words of Roy Charlton, president of the National Pony Society, 'the most famous of all sires of the general utility pony of that day, besides being the sire of pony stallions that quickly made pony history'.

Wilson ardently believed that by in-breeding his ponies, sire to daughter, he could impress upon them the stamp and action of Sir George. This policy also discouraged the ponies from growing any bigger, and minimised the risk of throw-backs to the full-size Hackneys from which Sir George was ultimately descended. To help guarantee the height restriction, foals were stabled for their first winter and then turned out on the Rigmaden moors to live as their native pony ancestors had done. The winter housing, in which they were cared for by Bob Moffatt, Wilson's experienced groom, consisted of fourteen stalls and several loose boxes arranged around a large

Although the Hackney pony was not standardised as a breed until the latter part of the nineteenth century, the type is now well established. Dennis Midgley driving Mr J. H. Chicken's national harness pony champion, Kiveton Manor George. (*Photo: Jim Moor*)

Hackney pony mares in winter, photographed at the Hart Hill Stud, Shaftesbury, owned by Neville Dent. (*Photo: Annie Dent*)

covered yard grandly called the riding school. Moffatt was responsible for all the stud work including foaling, handling the youngstock, and eventually breaking and schooling the ponies.

One of the first foals born at Rigmaden was a filly by Sir George and out of The Pet. She was born with a film covering one nostril which Bob Moffatt cut away, although shreds of it remained and caused her to make a snoring noise when trotting – hence her name, Snorer. She was a very weakly foal and Christopher Wilson gave orders for her to be put down, but unknown to her owner Moffatt took the foal back to his house, where he managed to save her, to the eventual surprise and delight of Wilson. She grew into an outstanding pony, winning at the Royal Show five years in succession and taking the gold medal presented by Queen Victoria at the Great Jubilee Show at Windsor in 1887. Mated back to Sir George, she bred Snorer II who, in the words of Vero Shaw, 'quite convinced Mr Wilson that his views upon the subject of close breeding and subsequent treatment were correct'. Two other daughters of Sir George, Georgina, whose dam was believed to be a Fell, and Lady Polo, were also mated back to their sire, and the resulting fillies covered by their grandfather again in due time. Thus the strain of ponies which for many years was simply known as the Wilson pony was established. Commenting on Wilson's breeding policy and in particular his success in standardising the height of his stock, Charles Richardson in his *Book of the Horse* wrote: 'C. W. Wilson's example should be imitated by those who have charge of youngstock; the latter must be turned out on poor land and generally experience a hard time of it if they appear likely to grow too big.' He went on to précis Wilson's theories into general advice:

1. Do not overlook the satisfactory results which can be derived from a judicious course of in-breeding.
2. Arrange that the foals are dropped later, in order that they and their dams do not enjoy all the best of the grass as the better the keep, the bigger the foal.
3. When foals are weaned put them on poor land, and do not over pamper them with warm housing.

With the increase of interest in Hackney ponies, many breeders began emulating Christopher Wilson's example and producing excellent stock by crossing Hackney stallions on to native pony mares, usually Welsh. Sir Gilbert Greenall was convinced that there was 'no doubt a great deal of Welsh blood in the Hackney pony'. It is interesting that the 13.2 hand dark brown pony stallion shown by the Stand Stud Company of Manchester under the name of Little Wonder, and a Royal Show winner, was out of a Welsh pony mare although his sire was the Hackney horse, D'Oyley's Confidence. Wilson sent Snorer to be mated by this pony and the result was a brown colt named Little Wonder II who in turn produced a wonderful pony called Sir Horace, believed by many to have had more influence on the Hackney pony breed than any other stallion including Sir George. Sir Horace won at the Hackney Society Show on seven occasions, the first time being in 1896 when one of the ringside spectators described the famous stallion and his progeny as having 'delightful pony features combined with speed and action'. At the 1904 London Hackney Show, not only was Sir Horace champion but six of the other eight prize winners in his class were by him, and his progeny won seven of the ten pony classes at the same show. 'With the advent of Sir Horace', Vero Shaw wrote, 'it may be said that the type of Hackney pony has become fixed, as there has never existed a more impressive sire, great or small.'

For many years the progeny of Sir Horace characterised the Hackney pony at its best. Sir Horace was out of a 13.3 hand mare by Lord Derby II which Wilson had bought as a brood mare. Although Lord Derby II was stated as being 15.2 hands, he was very probably considerably less. Wilson's other foundation mares by Sir George were equally successful, Georgina producing a long line of ponies all bearing her name, and Lady Polo breeding some excellent foals to Sir George including Winnal George, foaled in 1878, who had a notable showring career before being retired to stud.

Not all the Hackney pony stallions of this time included a percentage of pony blood, however. One of the most famous, Cassius, was by Cadet, a son of Lord Derby II, out of a full-size mare by D'Oyley's Confidence. Bred in 1886 by C. E. Cooke of Litcham in Norfolk, Cassius won the pony stallion class at the 1891 London Hackney Show and was champion at the Royal Show later that year. Despite having horse parentage and a full brother standing 15.3 hands, Cassius was well under fourteen hands, and the fact that he consistently bred stock of similar size helped make him one of the most important foundation sires of the breed.

Apart from Little Wonder mentioned above, other good Hackney ponies of the day included Lord Calthorpe's Don Carlos, whose dam, Corinna, was Welsh-bred; Lord Nimrod, a grandson of D'Oyley's Confidence out of a bay Welsh mare; and G. H. K. Francis' black pony, Pomfret Wonder, whose grandsire was Welsh. Many of the best Welsh mares for the purpose were by a stallion called Eidwen Flyer, who was believed to be a pure-bred Hackney horse and who was registered in the Hackney Stud Book, although he consistently bred under-sized foals, not a few of which were passed off as pure Welsh.

It was these little mares that were much in demand by early Hackney pony breeders. Roy Charlton recalled a conversation he had with Bob Moffatt following a sale of ponies at the Marquis of Londonderry's stud farm at Seaham Harbour, County Durham, in September 1896. Moffatt commented on the breeding of a brood mare just bought by Charlton. 'That little mare's dam, Firefly', Moffatt said, 'is by Cymro Lloyd, the Marshland Shales of Welsh ponies. Cymro Lloyd was the sire of King Jack, sire of Black Bess, dam of Eidwen Flyer II.' The Welsh and Hackney pony links were indisputable.

In marked contrast to the variety of colours which the Hackney horse was bred in, nearly all of the ponies bred by Christopher Wilson were bays with few or no white markings, and bay and brown were destined to become the most common colours for the Hackney pony breed. There were exceptions. The famous pony stallion, Cassius, was chestnut, his colour being inherited from his Hackney horse parentage, as 80 per cent of Hackney horses were chestnut at the time. There were also examples of grey Hackney ponies, the colour being traceable in most cases to Welsh pony ancestors,

51

Mrs Griselda McDonald's Hackney pony, Kippen Kaimsman, winner of many harness classes, including flying the flag for Hackney ponies in private driving classes and standing reserve in the Sanders Watney Memorial Championship in 1986. (*Photo: Jim Moor*)

as well as occasional roans, and the reserve breed champion at the 1917 Hackney Show, Harviestoun Wattie, was a dun.

From the start, Wilson operated a strict culling regime for any ponies he deemed to be of inferior standard, and Jonty Wilson, the Kirkby Lonsdale blacksmith, recalled that at the local show they had a better tradesman's turnout class than 'anywhere else in the country, many animals being throwouts from the famous Rigmaden stables'.

One morning in 1892 Christopher Wilson walked into the vast stableyard between the old house and the home farm and unexpectedly announced to his stud groom that he was selling all his ponies. He probably felt he had achieved all he had originally set out to do and it was time he moved on to something else. The best of the ponies were sold to the Marquis of Londonderry, Sir Gilbert Greenall and Sir Humphrey de Trafford, the latter also employing the services of Bob Moffatt. A few years later on

5 September 1895, Sir Humphrey's ponies were sold by public auction at Florden, Norfolk, when they made astronomical prices, breaking all previous records and turning the eyes of the equestrian world on to the Hackney pony. Miss Sniff, a bay yearling filly by Cassius out of Snorer II, topped the market at 900 guineas; Dorothy Derby, an eight-year-old 14 hand mare, made 600 guineas; her daughter, Dorothy Derby II, went under the hammer for 720 guineas; and Dorothy Derby II's yearling colt, Julius Caesar II, sold for 210 guineas. Snorer II, then an eight year old, fetched 600 guineas; her daughter, Snorer III, brought 700 guineas; and Georgina V, who like her dam and grandam was by Sir George, was sold for 700 guineas. Many of the ponies were bought by Sir Gilbert Greenall, who had joined the Hackney Horse Society the previous year, and used as foundation stock for his Tissington Stud in Derbyshire. He later acquired the famous Wilson-bred stallion, Sir Horace, on the death of the owner, A. J. Scott of Hampshire, who had purchased him privately from Sir Humphrey de Trafford prior to the latter's much publicised sale.

Although Christopher Wilson never returned to pony breeding, he maintained a distant interest in the Hackney pony by acting as an adviser to several new breeders including Sir Gilbert Greenall, and also judging occasionally, including once at the Hackney Show. Sir George, his famous old stallion, ended his days in the park at Rigmaden, and his tail now hangs as a memento over the fireplace of one of Christopher Wilson's great grandsons.

The popularity of the Hackney pony, fuelled by the high prices recorded at Sir Humphrey de Trafford's sale, encouraged other enthusiasts to set up studs, including Walter Cliff, a wealthy Yorkshire manufacturer, who began breeding ponies at the end of the last century. He began with two brown mares by Wildfire, a Hackney horse stallion, out of unknown dams although they were most probably of pony breeding. Put to Berkeley Model, a leading Hackney pony stallion of the day, one of the mares produced a filly foal named Success II who proved to be a great brood mare and the dam of some of the best ponies bred at Cliff's Melbourne Stud where, according to an advertisement of 1913, there was 'always a large selection of ponies for sale'.

Berkeley Model was owned by Alfred S. Day, a Cheshire veterinary chemist, who first became involved with Hackney ponies around 1892. He bought the four-year-old, brown-black stallion at the 1893 Hackney Show and changed his name prefix from Heacham to Berkeley, the name of Day's Crewe-based stud. Model was a grandson of D'Oyley's Confidence, the brown 15.2 hand stallion of Norfolk breeding whose illustrious progeny included Reality, champion of the first London Hackney Show. It was, however, Hackney ponies that Confidence was to have most

From the handful of Hackney pony breeders a little over a century ago, a succession of successful studs have been formed of which Messrs Neachell's Woodside Stud is one. Mr J. Wenham's champion harness pony of the 1980s, Woodside Kasper, driven by Jimmy Wenham, Jr. (*Photo: Jim Moor*)

influence on as he, like Lord Derby II, threw a percentage of pony-sized progeny in the first and subsequent generations. Berkeley Model was champion at the 1894 Hackney Show, and the following year he won again, beating Sir Horace into second place, the only time the famous stallion was ever beaten in the showring. Soon after this double success, Day purchased the rest of Berkeley Model's family and embarked on a successful in-breeding programme. When Berkeley Model died in 1900 at the age of only eleven, his place was taken by a pony called Fireboy, whose pedigree included Julius Caesar II (his sire), Cassius, Lord Derby II and D'Oyley's Confidence. When Alfred Day died in 1905 the Berkeley Stud was dispersed, but Walter Cliff's Melbourne Stud was to survive until the end of the First World War by which time it had contributed greatly to the improvement and standardisation of the Hackney pony. One of Walter Cliff's most influential ponies was a home-bred brood mare named Wortley Bell, a daughter of Sir Horace, and the dam of some of the top harness ponies of the day.

Other notable Hackney pony studs of the time included J. Ernest Kerr's Harviestoun Stud up in Scotland, where the great pony stallion, Sir Horace, ended his days in 1917, and Mr and Mrs Alfred C. King's Braishfield Stud in the New Forest, where the dun stallion Harviestoun Wattie stood for several years. Stock from Sir Gilbert Greenall's Tissington Stud had been used to found the Harviestoun Stud, while at Braishfield much of the foundation stock had been of Walter Cliff's Melbourne bloodline.

Although there had always been a class for ponies shown in harness at the annual Hackney Show held in London, the schedule was extended in 1906 to include classes for harness ponies under 13 hands, from 13 to 13.2 hands, and up to but not exceeding 14 hands, as well as a harness pony championship. The revised classification was agreed by the Hackney Horse Society council members and show organisers in response to the increasing popularity of Hackney ponies and in particular the exhibiting of ponies in harness. The new championship was won that year by Tissington Kit Kat, bred by Sir Gilbert Greenall, and sired by Sir Horace out of a Wilson-bred mare

Mrs Elspeth Gill driving her pony, Finesse, to a spider phaeton, which was the favoured four-wheel vehicle for exhibiting Hackneys in the early years of the London Hackney Show. (*Photo: Jim Moor*)

called Lady Kate. Although there were many amateurs and professionals showing Hackney ponies in harness, the leading exhibitor was William Foster of Moseley, Warwickshire, whose Mel-Vally stables turned out a succession of top class harness ponies. His famous four-in-hand of bay Hackney ponies won the harness championship at the International Horse Show in 1908. This team of 13.2 hand geldings, which consisted of two grandsons of Cassius, a son of Sir Horace and a son of Goldstone, was later sold along with its fine pony-size coach and team harness to Alfred G. Vanderbilt, the American industrial magnate, for £5,000. The following year, when William Foster won the harness championship at the Hackney Show with a pony bred by Sir Gilbert Greenall, Tissington Belief, the pony harness classes had become amongst the most popular with spectators at the shows.

Although the Hackney Horse Society initially recommended a height limit of 14.2 hands for ponies, this was later reduced to 14 hands. In the best examples the head is small and shows masses of quality and pony character with a bold, kind eye and small ears. A large, plain or coarse head is out of character for what is essentially a pony

The Hon. Mrs N. Ionides' famous Hackney pony stallion, Highstone Nicholas, driven by Cynthia Haydon, 1960. As well as having a successful showring career, this pony bred many champions. (*Photo: Jim Moor*)

Miss R. S. Davidson's successful Hackney pony stallion, Marden Finality, shown by Jimmy Davies. Finality was by Highstone Nicholas. (*Photo: Jim Moor*)

breed. The well-formed and muscular neck should show a good top-line, a tendency to crestiness being preferable to weakness between the poll and withers, and the shoulder should be well laid back. The carcase should be deep with plenty of heart room and well-sprung ribs, and the quarters should be strong and muscular with the tail well set on. The legs are strong with adequate bone for the size of animal, short cannon bones and well-let-down hocks, and the hoofs are well-shaped and hard. The overall appearance should suggest boldness, enthusiasm, activity and tremendous character coupled with boundless presence – an essential attribute of any show animal. The action of the Hackney pony is distinctive for, unlike the slower cadence associated with the Hackney horse, the walk is springy and crisp, and the trot spectacular and animated with extravagant knee and hock action but without the loss of ground-covering ability. Self-assured, alert and bursting with energy, they should, as the old horse dealers would say, 'fill the eye'.

The Hackney pony, like most other breeds, suffered during the bleak years of the

First World War. When, in peace time, the shows were revived the new generation of animals which emerged to contend the Hackney pony classes were evolving into a different stamp of animal. In an attempt to produce ponies with more exaggerated action, much of the bone and substance of the old type of Hackney pony was being lost, along with the inherent stamina for which these ponies were once famous. The 'narrow-gutted flying machines', as one observer disparagingly described them, were also more highly couraged and neurotic than their more equable natured predecessors had been. As Roy Charlton wrote:

> the speed with which Hackney ponies changed from real ponies into absolute monstrosities was simply astonishing . . . immediately after the Great War, I went once, only once, to the Hackney Show at Doncaster, to be extremely disappointed with the dreadful-looking animals that were shown as Hackney ponies.

Fortunately, the breed's total decline was prevented by those breeders who held on to the old bloodlines, so that when Roy Charlton, writing in 1937 about the better standard of ponies he had seen exhibited at Olympia and the Richmond Horse Show, expressed the hope that the Hackney pony's worst years were over, his optimism was almost prophetic. Even so, the pony stallion championship at the following year's Hackney Show was won by an American-bred pony, Stonehedge Brigadier, while the champion harness pony at the same show, Nigel Colman's Cassilis High and Mighty, was another American import.

5 The Hurstwood Stud

Of the many important Hackney studs of the post-war period, one has been particularly influential and that is the Hurstwood Stud owned by Frank and Cynthia Haydon. Founded in 1945, the stud is unique in that it has not only bred a succession of champion horses and ponies but it has also distinguished itself in the training, production and showing of Hackneys. Since 1946 when the Hurstwood Stud first exhibited at the Hackney Horse Society Show at Crewe, it has dominated the showring, and the Haydons are universally acknowledged as the most experienced breeders and exhibitors of Hackneys in the world.

Cynthia Haydon's involvement with Hackneys began at a very early age as her father, Robert Black, was the most successful Hackney trainer of his day and, in partnership with his brother James, he ran a thriving public training yard at Osbaldwick, near York. The brothers moved to Reading in 1932 where they each ran their own stables, so Cynthia grew up surrounded by Hackneys and, whilst still in her teens, made her showring debut with a team of ponies belonging to Bertram Mills. The circus proprietor and coaching enthusiast had personally trained Cynthia for the job, and she proved herself an apt pupil as her later successes were to show. She later recalled that on her first outing with the team she was so nervous that she dropped the reins when about to enter the ring but, control restored, she drove with great success and thereafter her showring career never looked back.

Frank Haydon first drove Hackneys for his father when in his early teens, so his involvement with the breed also began early. He married Cynthia shortly after the war and they set up a Hackney breeding farm and public training stable at Sleeches Farm, High Hurstwood, Uckfield, in 1945, later moving to Shovelstrode Farm, near East Grinstead, as the stud expanded in size. From the very start the stud benefited from the advice and guidance of Robert Black who, although retired, maintained a keen interest in the breed. It was he who purchased, among others, the great stallion Solitude at Joe Morton's dispersal sale in 1940, and ultimately sent him to Hurstwood where he played a significant role in establishing the reputation of the stud. Solitude, a 15.1 hand bay horse, was foaled in 1933 and was by Buckley Courage out of a grand-daughter of Matthias called Dark Vision. Unshown by his breeder, Joe Morton, due to the war, his first appearance in the showring was at the Hackney Horse Society Show at Crewe in 1946 when, in the ownership of the Haydons, he won his class, the stallion championship, and the supreme championship of the show.

He repeated this success in 1947 and 1948 before being retired to stud, as he was then fifteen years old and his owners considered his future as a breeding stallion to be of greater importance than a continuation of his showring career.

Most of Solitude's progeny possessed action, one of his first foals to achieve fame being the 14.3 hand mare, Holywell Florette. She was bred by Claude Goddard, a past president of the Hackney Horse Society, out of a good mare called Lavington Flavia. When Mr Goddard died in 1945, his stock was sold at a dispersal sale and Florette, then a rather unimpressive two year old, was bought by W. T. Barton of Redhill for 300 guineas. Despite a report in the equestrian press after the sale describing Florette as the bargain of the day, Mr Barton later doubted the wisdom of his impetuous purchase and it was not until he sent her to the Haydons to be broken and produced for the showring that she began to show any real potential. A slow maturer, she was only lightly shown as a three year old, but the following year in 1948 she returned to the showring in earnest and swept all before her as she won championships at all the leading shows including Windsor, the Royal, the Hackney Show, and the Royal International Horse Show. Driven by Cynthia Haydon, this very stylish liver chestnut mare with four white stockings and a blaze found favour with virtually all judges, who liked her free-going and scopey action and great presence. She was retired to stud as a nine-year-old after a show career of outstanding success.

In later years, when Frank Haydon was asked in an interview if any particular horse he had shown stood out in is memory, he said it would have to be Solitude, and many of today's top Hackneys can be traced back to him.

Another cornerstone of the Hurstwood Stud was the 15 hand bay mare, Erlegh Maiden, bred by Robert Black, and out of his good mare, Allerthorpe Carnation, by Nork Spotlight, a young but very promising stallion. Spotlight, foaled in 1931 and a son of Mersey Searchlight, was reserve supreme champion at the Hackney Show as a two year old, and he repeated this success the following year when his famous father took top honours. Erlegh Maiden caused a sensation when she won the yearling class, the junior championship, and was reserve champion female at the Hackney Show in 1935. She was then sold to Mrs R. H. McColl, in whose ownership she won her class and the junior championship at the Hackney Show the following year and also took the overall female championship. In 1937 she enjoyed another field day at the Hackney Show, and twelve months later she added the in-hand championship and novice harness reserve championship to her growing list of honours. Her show career prospered with wins at Olympia and other major shows, and early in 1944 Frank Haydon managed to purchase her through his father-in-law, who had bred her, from the executors of the McColl estate. She was in foal to Solitude at the time and later that spring produced Hurstwood Supremo, whose many wins included standing reserve supreme champion to his sire, Solitude, at the Hackney Show one year. As a six year old, Supremo was exported to the United States.

In 1945 Erlegh Maiden foaled to Solitude again, a colt called Hurstwood Commander who, although seldom shown due to an injury received as a foal, bred some excellent stock which earned him first place in the produce group class at the 1954 Hackney Show. One of his first foals, Hurstwood Creation, was exported to Australia where he won at the Sydney Show. In 1946, Erlegh Maiden produced a filly, Hurstwood Lonely Lady, again by Solitude. Lonely Lady was female supreme champion at the Hackney Show as both a yearling and two year old, and in later years was champion harness horse at Harringay and, in the experienced hands of Dick Midgley, supreme champion harness horse at the Hackney Show.

Erlegh Maiden's 1947 foal, another filly, Hurstwood Lonely Maid, continued to keep the Hurstwood prefix in the forefront of the Hackney world by prolific wins, including supreme female champion at the Hackney Show in 1949. Several years later she was exported to Canada. Solitude's fifth foal out of Erlegh Maiden was Hurstwood Superlative, a temperamental but brilliant bay mare of just over 15.1 hands who was not shown until she was five, by which time she had bred a colt,

Noddy Vyse driving Mrs E. E. Vyse's Whitehavens Step High, a champion whose bloodlines trace back to Solitude and Erlegh Maiden. (*Photo: Jim Moor*)

Hurstwood Consul, who was three times junior champion at the Hackney Show. Superlative's harness debut was at the Royal Windsor Show in 1953 where she won the supreme championship, and she went on to win at the Richmond Horse Show, the Royal, and the Hackney Show, finishing the season unbeaten. Driven by Cynthia Haydon, she swept the board in harness classes for the next few years, and was supreme champion harness horse in 1955.

Erlegh Maiden lost her foals in 1949 and 1950 but her 1951 filly, Hurstwood Demoiselle, by Walton Diplomat, was twice supreme champion mare at the Hackney Show, and Demoiselle's younger sister, Hurstwood Donazella, won both as a yearling and as a two year old. Erlegh Maiden died in 1954 having left a string of top-class progeny with the Hurstwood prefix and made her mark on the Hackney breed.

The Haydons did not restrict the breeding side of Hurstwood to horses only, and many top-class Hackney ponies were bred with the famous prefix including Hurstwood Consort, champion pony stallion from 1976 to 1984 and again in 1986.

Consort, a son of the illustrious stallion, Highstone Nicholas, also won in harness at the Royal International Horse Show and the Horse of the Year Show before being retired to stud. Mrs Haydon showed the home-bred pony, Hurstwood Untouchable, a grandson of Highstone Nicholas, for his owner, Miss R. S. Davidson, with huge success in the early 1980s. Visiting mares are taken to both the Hackney horse and pony stallions and a Thoroughbred stallion standing at stud at Hurstwood.

Although Frank Haydon once described his and Cynthia's main occupation as the production of Hackney horses and ponies, this objective would have to include the training and exhibition of animals. In addition to home-bred stock, the Haydons

Miss R. S. Davidson's two pony stallions: Hurstwood Consort (*opposite page*), the champion pony stallion for the years 1976–84 and again in 1986; and (*below*) Hurstwood Untouchable, a great-grandson of Highstone Nicholas, driven here by Cynthia Haydon. (*Photos: Jim Moor*)

63

break, school and produce to a very high standard many show animals for other owners, a policy they have pursued since the early years of the stud, and their phenomenal success over many years has guaranteed a following of satisfied customers. In the 1970s the stud moved from Shovelstrode Farm because the surrounding area was becoming too built up, which made the driving of horses in close proximity of the farm difficult. A new home was found at Manor Farm, Lower Slaughter in the Cotswolds, which was central for travelling to the major shows, and the nearby Roman roads from which motor vehicles are debarred were ideal for the driving of horses. In later years the stud moved to Addlestrop, again in the Cotswolds.

The innumerable champions produced by the Haydons for other owners and driven by Cynthia in the showring included Walton Diplomat owned by W. T. Barton, who hoped the young stallion might make a showring replacement for his great mare, Holywell Florette. A beautifully made but highly couraged horse, Diplomat's first outing in the ring at Windsor in 1951 was marred, as the four year old refused to settle and he was placed second to Hurstwood Lonely Lady. Despite the advice of others to geld him, the Haydons persevered and he was unbeaten for the rest of that season, and two years later justified their convictions by winning the supreme harness horse championship. This ability to produce horses to realise their full potential earned the Haydons great respect, and a succession of owners including Captain R. S. de Quincey, the Misses Davidson, Mr and Mrs J. A. McDougald, and Mr Chauncey Stillman sought the Haydon's services to show their animals.

In 1949 Mrs Harcourt-Wood sent her 11.2 hand, nine-year-old dark brown Hackney pony, Bossy, to the Haydons as, after some good wins in novice classes, he appeared to be making little progress in open classes. In Mrs Haydon's skilled hands, he won the harness pony championship at the Richmond Horse Show and the supreme championship at the Hackney Show and was rarely beaten for the rest of that season. Sold on to new owners, he amassed over 1,000 prizes before being retired.

Another of Mrs Haydon's successes was the pony stallion, Oakwell Sir James, which she first produced in harness in 1950 for his owner, Miss M. P. James, winning the novice pony championships at the Hackney Show. Shown from his owner's stable for the next two years, he returned to the Hurstwood Stud in 1953, winning nine firsts and six championships that season, and the following year he increased his winnings to seventeen firsts and twelve championships, including the harness pony supreme championship at the Hackney Show. Bought by Frank Haydon that autumn, he was sold to the Hon. Mrs N. Ionides for whom he won consistently.

On over forty-five occasions, Mrs Haydon won the horse or pony harness championship, an amazing achievement, as well as clocking up numerous other showring

The Hon. Mrs N. Ionides' stallion, Oakwell Sir James, shown by Jimmy Davies. Sir James was champion pony in hand at the Hackney Show, 1952–6, as well as a big winner in harness. He stood 12.1½ hands. (*Photo: Jim Moor*)

successes both in this country as well as in America and Canada where the Haydons showed regularly.

In looking back over the years to the outstanding Hackneys which have helped mould the breed and popularise it, few are either unrelated to Hurstwood stock or were not shown by the Haydons at some point in their careers. Many were supplied by the Haydons who bought animals on commission for clients. Harlock Chiquita, the champion harness pony of 1946 to 1948, was one of these. Originally shown by Mrs Haydon on behalf of her owner, Mr T. Neal, she was bought by Frank Haydon in 1946 and sold on to Mrs B. H. Mellor for whom she won prolifically. Many Hurstwood-bred or bought-in animals were also exported around the world, a great many going to the United States.

The Haydon's competitive activities also extended to coaching classes, and they enjoyed considerable success showing Mr and Mrs J. A. McDougald's team of bay Hackneys to a park drag in the 1970s. The same team was also driven by Mrs Haydon in international driving trials, where their many successes included a team gold medal for Britain.

Perhaps the most long-term of the Haydon's many achievements is their overall marketing of the Hackney breed and its capabilities, and in this respect they have no peers. Mrs Haydon, who was awarded the MBE for her services to the equestrian world, was elected president of the Hackney Horse Society in 1986 and although she and her husband have now curtailed their showing and Hackney breeding activities they are still involved in instructing and training pupils, and they maintain a keen interest in the breed they have done so much to further.

6 The Hackney abroad and its influence on other breeds

In the early years of the nineteenth century, the Hackney first came to the attention of French horse breeders. They recognised in the breed the qualities they sought to introduce into their native mares to produce a better class of horse for the road and for the military. From the first few Hackneys purchased and shipped out to France in the 1830s, a substantial international export trade in British horses grew which eventually extended to countries in all four corners of the world and which was to last well into the twentieth century.

The French breeders and dealers who initiated the trade found no difficulty in procuring Hackneys, for by the time their purchasing forays into the eastern counties were well established the agricultural depression of 1835–45 was forcing many farmers to sell their stock, making the foreign buyers especially welcome. As the new age of the railway brought the coaching era to a close there was a real concern that harness horses would soon be unwanted and unsaleable. Consequently the Frenchmen were well pleased to be offered Hackneys which were not only of top quality but also competitively priced, and before long English agents were being recruited to act as buyers for both European governments and private individuals. One such buyer, a man named Hetherington who purchased Hackney stallions on behalf of the horse-breeding department of the French government for over a quarter of a century, said of Hackneys: 'they are very popular with the breeders; they are used in preference to the Thoroughbred, and improve their horses more than anything'. He was responsible for exporting upwards of thirty stallions each year and he was only one of many dealers involved in this lucrative trade. One of the innumerable good horses sent to France was St Giles, a stallion bred in Yorkshire by F. Rickell in 1858 and exhibited as a six year old at the Paris Exhibition where he won first prize.

Sir Walter Gilbey wrote that 'the success of the French in establishing a breed of road-horses from a foundation of Hackney blood is nowhere more noteworthy than in Normandy', and soon the horses of the Morleraut district which were sired by English stallions were held in high repute for use both on the roads and as artillery horses. By the end of the nineteenth century these Anglo-Norman horses were being bred in large numbers and, as Gilbey went on, 'their superiority is so unanimously recognised that government agents of Austria, Hungary, and most other continental nations regularly visited Normandy to purchase their stallions'. Monsieur de Thannberg, an adviser to the French government on horse-breeding, summed up the value of the Hackney imports when he said: 'although these horses are not very high bred, they are of very similar conformation. They invariably transmit to their off-spring all their qualities, their action, their courage – in one word, all that constitutes the requisites for a good troop horse.'

The Breton horse, a draught/agricultural breed originating on the poor land of Brittany, was also influenced by imported Hackney blood in the nineteenth century. Strong, hardy, and with the ability to thrive on poor keep, the Breton horse crossed well with the Hackney, and a lighter type of Breton horse known as the Breton Postier was developed in the interior of the Brittany region. Standing between 15 and 16 hands in height, the Breton Postier was an excellent mover and much in demand for road work.

Encouraged by the success of the imported stallions, the trade had been extended to breeding mares too and, as an increasing number of Hackneys crossed the channel, concerns began to be voiced as to the impact this was having on the breeding stock left in England. A House of Commons Select Committee was formed to address the situation in 1873, and Joshua East, a dealer and one of the biggest London job-masters who always had around 1,000 carriage horses in his stables, advised the committee that French agents 'buy the very best and they get mares. You cannot get them to buy a bad mare.' Anglo-Norman horses, some of which were actually pure Hackney, were even being sold back across the channel and Colonel Connolly, military attaché to the British Embassy in Paris, said that the French remount officers 'complain very much of all their best Norman horses going to England for carriage horses!' If nothing else, the Select Committee's work drew attention to the value of the Hackney as a national resource, and Sir Walter Gilbey in his book, *The Harness Horse* (1898), wrote optimistically: 'We still possess the very best of the old Hackney breeding stock, and though it is as yet more remarkable for quality than quantity its numerical strength increases yearly, thanks largely to the exertions of the Hackney Horse Society during the fifteen years of its existence.'

The French were not the only nation decimating the numbers of Hackneys in England through their imports, however. Buyers from the Italian government had been coming to Norfolk and Lincolnshire since around 1850, purchasing Hackney stallions to breed on to local mares to produce horses for military purposes. The numbers bought fluctuated from year to year, with only sixteen stallions imported in 1888 while seventy stallions made the trip to Italy in 1890. The following year the Master of Horse of the Italian Government was instructed to purchase 600 Hackney stallions,

100 a year for six years in succession, but the contract never materialised. The trade continued up until 1933 when the last Hackney stallion to be purchased by the Italian authorities left these shores. As few Hackney mares were imported and the stallions were specifically used for cross-breeding, as soon as the government was no longer involved in breeding horses for the military the Hackney fell from prominence and, despite occasional imports of harness horses in more recent times, there has never been great interest in pure-bred Hackneys in Italy.

The same applied to Germany where, on the advice of H. R. Phillips, the famous London horse-dealer, a number of Hackneys were imported during the latter half of the nineteenth century and used in several breeding districts under the auspices of the government. The Hackneys were preferred to the earlier imports of Cleveland Bays and Yorkshire Coach Horses and, while few were bred pure in Germany, their influence on the local breeds which had developed from the Great War Horse of Europe was significant. Breeds like the Oldenburg, which was strong but lacking in hardiness and endurance, benefited from the Hackney blood, which also found its way into the Holstein breed and, to a lesser extent, the Hanoverian.

Between 1878 and 1889, Hackneys were imported to Radautz, the former state-owned stud of the Austro-Hungarian Empire, later situated in the former Yugoslavia, and English horses of the 'Norfolk-type' were among the breeding mares at the Piber stud, now home of the Austrian Lipizzaners, around 1800. A stallion of Norfolk-type called Great Gun was also used at the stud for a time.

In Finland around the middle of the last century, much attention was given to the question of how to give the indigenous horses more strength, size and weight and, although Thoroughbred, Arab and Orlov Trotter imports were considered, after considerable and heated discussion the Hackney was the breed selected, and a number of stallions and mares were brought over from the Norfolk region. The policy was not unsuccessful but it was not repeated, and selective in-breeding was favoured for further experimental improvement programmes.

In 1860 Colonel Frederick Barlow of Woodbridge in Suffolk was reputedly instrumental in introducing East European breeders directly to the Hackney when he sold his six-year-old stallion, North Star, to the Austro-Hungarian government. A grandson of Ramsdale's Wildfire, North Star was believed to have been sent to the government breeding farm at Mezohegyes where a programme to produce a dual-purpose utility type of animal had been initiated some twenty years earlier using an English Thoroughbred stallion. However, in 1852 General Ritter had bought on behalf of the Austrian government an English Thoroughbred stallion called North Star, bred by Lord Fitzwilliam and foaled in 1844, and there seems to be some confusion over which of the North Stars was successful in founding the distinct strain of warm-blood horses still known in Hungary by the North Star name. Whichever horse it was, some of the best Hungarian-bred horses of today can be traced back to him.

In India in 1876, the Department of Horse Breeding Operations and the Remount Department who worked in partnership to ensure a plentiful supply of quality remounts for the British Army imported 300 stallions of different breeds and types to 'gain greater size and power in the produce of country-bred mares', many of whom stood little more than 13.2 hands. Ten years later when the success of the various breeds imported could be assessed against the quality of stock being produced, the Hackney came out on top. Consequently, the stallions employed in the breeding programmes in 1886 comprised 1 Persian, 2 Turkoman, 6 Australian Thoroughbreds, 10 cross-breds, 90 English Thoroughbreds, 146 Arabs, but 159 Hackneys, all of which were scattered throughout the horse-breeding districts, where they were used only on those mares approved as being of a suitable type and branded to show eligibility for a free service by one of the Government stallions. As there were 20,000 of these branded mares in India, a large number of part-bred Hackneys were obviously being bred. Gilbey, writing in his book *Horse Breeding in England and India and Army Horses Abroad* (1901), comments that between 1886 and 1892 figures gathered from the horse-breeding districts and showing the percentage of prize-winners sired by stallions of the various breeds at the district shows easily puts the Hackney first and well ahead of the Thoroughbred. The progeny of Hackneys also appeared to acclimatise to the heat better than the progeny of Thoroughbreds or other breeds, a characteristic that was recognised in other parts of the world where the Hackney was being used to produce utility half-breds.

The Hackney was not always successful in improving the native stock of other countries, however, and an attempt to upgrade the horses of South Africa, including the Basuto pony, by importing twenty-eight Hackney stallions in 1888, achieved little and was not repeated by the Cape Colony government. Private individuals, whose prospecting activities had brought them considerable wealth in a short time, were more enthusiastic as they liked to be seen behind a smart stepping horse, and they made further imports. The first months of the Boer War in 1899 saw more pure and part-bred Hackneys shipped out to South Africa, and there is evidence of heavy cavalry horses, bred in Russia but by imported English Hackney stallions, being sold back to the British government for use in the South African War. One squadron of the Imperial Yeomanry recruited in East Anglia was mounted on Hackneys bred in that area, and according to a report in the *Livestock Journal*, they withstood the hardships of the campaign better than most of the other imported English horses. It is probable that the renewed interest in the Hackney after the war was largely due to its commendable performance during the hostilities, and considerable numbers were imported under a new government scheme which survived up until the 1950s and under which the freight charges for approved livestock were paid. Although most of the horses brought in under the scheme were for cross-breeding, some were used to establish pure-bred studs, but it was not until the 1940s when a group of breeders in the Orange Free State imported seventeen more English Hackneys over a period of three years that interest in the breed was really revived. Their example was emulated by other enthusiasts in the years that followed as the breeding and exhibiting of harness horses increased in popularity, and in 1961 the first Hackney ponies were imported when Mrs Wessels purchased two ponies from the famous Hurstwood Stud. In due course these were joined by other ponies including several American-bred animals, and today both horses and ponies are well established in South Africa with strong Hackney classes at most of the shows and an active breed society responsible for the registration of stock.

In 1891, a stallion called Carat became the first Hackney to be imported into New Zealand when he was purchased by Mr Teschmaker of Canterbury. Ten years later, Galantine, another stallion, was shipped to Rangitikei in North Island, and in 1903 the first of a succession of imports was made into South Island where these stallions were used to breed cross-breds for saddle and harness work. A few Hackney ponies were later imported but interest in the breed waned after the Second World War, and it was not until the 1970s that both Hackney horses and ponies came back into popularity in a big way. Considerable numbers of Hackneys were imported from England and also Australia, especially in the 1980s, and there are now many well-established studs of high quality throughout New Zealand, and Hackney classes are included at most of the larger shows where they are very popular with spectators.

In 1903, Captain Phillip Charley, an Australian fighting in the Boer War, came to England where he bought and subsequently took home to Australia two well-bred Hackney stallions to use on native mares. The stamina demonstrated by the Hackneys in the service of the British in South Africa may have prompted him to make his purchases and, although they were not the first Hackneys to land on Australian soil, they created some interest and a few more were imported in the years up until the First World War. It was not until the 1950s, however, that the Hackney horse as a show harness breed was re-discovered in Australia, and breeders like Tom Dwyer of New South Wales were among the first to import fresh bloodlines of top quality with which to establish the breed on a permanent basis.

At the same time as Captain Charley was importing his first horses, R. G. Wilson

Mr Roger Bass' consistent prize winner, Forewood Commander, driven by Georgina Turner. This horse was sold to Holland in 1993. (*Photo: Jim Moor*)

of Melbourne introduced into Australia the first Hackney pony, Berkeley Magician, and soon afterwards several ponies from Sir Gilbert Greenall's stud went to a breeder in Sydney, followed by a string of other imports as the Australians, to whom ponies were something of a novelty, delighted in these little Hackneys. Despite their immense popularity, by the end of the Second World War their numbers had dwindled to a handful.

In 1946, Cliff Thackeray imported Marfleet Cadet, a brown pony stallion, who was to revive the fortunes of the breed in Australia. Several New Zealand-bred mares by an English-bred pony stallion, Glenavon Torchstar, together with a few imported English pony mares were shipped in as foundation stock for Thackeray's stud, which up until his death in 1957 produced ponies which swept the board annually in the harness classes at the Royal Sydney Show. Not only did he popularise the breed, he encouraged other enthusiasts who took up the baton and continued the breed's rise in popularity until the Hackney pony now outnumbers his larger counterpart. An Australian breed society oversees registrations.

In recent years the Australians' fascination with ponies has resulted in the development of a new national breed of pony known simply as the Australian pony and largely founded on Welsh and Hackney pony blood. Ideally suited to both saddle and harness work, its success re-affirms the values of the Hackney as a crossing sire.

In 1900 the Japanese government began importing English-bred Hackney stallions on an annual basis to upgrade the quality of cavalry horses bred at their remount breeding farms. The trade petered out in the 1920s, with the exception of one purchase of six Hackney ponies from the Hurstwood Stud in 1965.

The Dutch have always been interested in trotting horses and there is little doubt that some of the very early ancestors of the Hackney originated in Holland. In 1903 Miss Ella Ross, an enthusiastic harness horse exhibitor, took her well-known black Hackneys over to Holland to show at the Hague Show. Their appearance generated much interest in the breed, with the result that several studs were founded there in the pre-war years including Baron Van Voorst tot Voorst's large breeding farm near Arnhem. By the time the Baron died in 1920, there was a nucleus of excellent breeding stock in the hands of several new enthusiasts and, supported with further imports, the breed numbers grew as harness classes became an important feature of many of the national shows. In 1946 the Netherlands Hackney Stud Book Society was formed and it has remained active ever since. Stallions and mares as well as youngstock are now inspected prior to registration and, although horses are more popular than ponies, both are bred in larger numbers than in Britain.

The Dutch Gelderlander horse, now very popular as a harness breed although originally produced for farm and saddle work, was standardised with the help of Hackney blood, which may account for its stylish action. Earlier this century, when the first Hackneys were imported into Holland, the Gelderland Breed Society accepted them into the Gelderland stud book provided they met the eligibility criteria of suitable size and type. In recent years a new type of horse known as the Dutch Harness Horse has been produced using Gelderland and Hackney stock, and stud book registrations for the new breed are maintained by the Dutch Warmblood Society.

The Groninger, a Dutch farm horse breed also sometimes used as a heavyweight saddle horse or for driving, was influenced in its early history by Norfolk Roadster blood. The Swiss Einsiedler breed, now a modern multi-purpose warmblood, also had strong early Roadster/Hackney connections, one of the most influential stallions being a Yorkshire-bred horse called Bracken, described as a roadster and bought in Basel in 1865.

The Yorkshire Trotter stallion, Bracken, was bought in Basel in 1865, and was a great influence on the Swiss Einsiedler breed.

In the latter part of the nineteenth century, the flourishing export trade in beef brought considerable wealth to the landowners and cattle barons of Argentina, many of whom owned palatial town houses in Buenos Aires, and it became fashionable to be seen driving in the streets and parks of the city. Expensive and stylish carriages and harness made by the finest European craftsmen were shipped in and, because the local Criollo ponies were neither big enough nor sufficiently flashy for park driving, Hackney horses were imported for the purpose. At a time when most other countries importing Hackneys did so for cross-breeding, Argentinians were among the few interested in breeding pure-bred Hackneys, and they have continued to do so up until the present day. Unlike most others, they bought as many mares as stallions which gave them sufficient breeding stock to form studs, and their purchases included some of the best horses available, such as Hawsker Rosina, the champion mare of 1907 and 1908, and Hopwood Viceroy, champion stallion of 1913. By the time the import trade was beginning to diminish around 1914, over 1,000 English-bred Hackneys had been imported and a breed registry had been in existence for seven years.

Although there were harness horse classes at the Palermo Show, the Argentinians' interest in the Hackney was not for the showring but for the road, with the effect that there was never any danger of a show type developing. Present-day Argentinian horses are, in the words of one breeder, 'old-fashioned or working Hackneys'. One of the largest Hackney breeders of earlier times was Señor Martinez de Hoz, owner of the Chapadmalal estancia, who in 1908 brought forty-five of his home-bred Hackneys to England to horse the 'Reliance' revival coach which he ran for the season between London and Guildford. The team who did the ten-mile stage between Cobham and Guildford were, in the words of Ted Fownes, the coachman, 'four lions', and Major-General Geoffrey White said of Martinez de Hoz's horses: 'those people who are

A mare of typical Argentinian Hackney type, Sissi, bred by Carlos Lattuada. (*Photo: S. Bailey*)

Two Argentinian-bred animals. The Hackney stallion, Spot (*above*), owned by Carlos Lattuada. He is directly descended from English Hackneys imported early in the twentieth century. In Argentinian tradition, his tail is docked. Sesostris (*below*), a yearling colt by Spot, demonstrates tremendous natural hock action. (*Photos: S. Bailey*)

prejudiced against the Hackney breed, and mistrustful of their powers of doing a journey, might have modified their opinions after a day spent behind these produce of the Argentine'. Only a handful of Hackneys have been exported from Britain to Argentina during the last fifty years, although two South American-bred horses were imported into Britain during 1992, but there are now a number of size-able studs in Argentina producing up to seventy foals per annum. With the growing popularity of harness competitions, particularly driving trials, the future of the Hackney there should be assured.

Hackneys were also imported into other South American countries including Uruguay, and in 1889 Colonel North presented the Hackney stallion, Copenhagen, to the Chilean government who later purchased two more stallions, but these were iso-lated imports.

In 1822, the Norfolk Roadster, Jary's Bellfounder, was shipped to Boston and although he was not the first of his breed to land in North America he was one of the most important. A descendant of the Darley Arabian, Bellfounder became the foun-dation sire of the American Standardbred trotter as well as one of the most celebrated horses of his day. Eight years later the Hudson Bay Company took the first recorded Hackney stallion into Canada, and in the years that followed large num-bers of English-bred Hackneys were shipped across the Atlantic with the aim of breeding better carriage and draught horses. The first stud of pure-bred Hackneys was founded in Canada in 1881. Two years later, Alexander J. Cassatt of Philadelphia, president of the Philadelphia Railroad, started the first stud in the United States when he purchased Little Wonder, the fourteen hand son of Reality and champion at the first London Hackney Show, and two mares by Lord Derby II. Writing in the American magazine, *Harpers Weekly*, on 9 April 1892, Cassatt announced:

It is only within the last ten years that the Hackney as a distinct breed became generally known in America. I believe my horse, Little Wonder, imported in January 1883, and exhibited at the first show of the National Horse Show Association in New York, and Mr Prescott Lawrence's grand mover, Fashion, imported one year later, were the first Hackneys that attracted public attention in the United States. Since then the breed has rapidly grown in favour.

His views were not shared by everyone and James Halfpenny, writing in *The Michigan Farmer*, believed that 'the so-called Hackney is nothing more than a light harness horse and there is no place that he can fill that our American trotter cannot discount him'. Another supporter of the American trotter writing in the *Chicago*

Cynthia Haydon drove a number of turnouts for Canadian owner Mrs J. A. McDougald. The Hackney horse team (*above*) competed in driving trials as well as coaching classes; two members of the team, Hurstwood Demolight and Le Fylde Popstar (*below*), were also driven in tandem to a gig. (*Photos: Jim Moor*)

Horseman on 6 August 1892 said: 'There never was a Hackney that could trot a mile in three minutes imported to this country.' Despite the cynicism of these and other writers, the Hackney flourished under the eye of the American Hackney Horse Society, formed in 1890 to establish and improve the Hackney breed and publish a stud book, the first volume of which contained the records of 80 stallions and 264 mares. Two years later in 1892 the Canadian Hackney Horse Society was formed, although the majority of Canadian Hackneys were still being used for cross-breeding with heavy mares, especially Clydesdales, to produce strong draught horses, some of which were exported back to Britain where the demand for horses was out-stripping the home-bred supply. At this time, American breeders were supplying the French with regular consignments of horses, '15.2 to 16 hands in height, free from hereditary unsoundness, and showing good action'. Most were out of draught mares by Hackney stallions, a cross that had proved very successful in Kentucky as well as Virginia where Henry Fairfax's Matchless of Londesboro' stood at stud. In New York and other cities along the eastern seaboard, the Hackney became the favoured breed for carriage work and park driving, while the half-bred Hackney proliferated among the tradesmen and delivery men who valued its stamina, strength and placid nature.

In rural Vermont the farmers were more reticent about change despite the work of Dr W. Seward Webb, a New York physician and Hackney enthusiast whose marriage in 1881 to Lila Vanderbilt, daughter of the multi-millionaire railway magnate, had instigated his move to New England. Following a visit in 1890 to the English stud of his fellow American, William Burdett-Coutts, Dr Webb imported a consignment of top-class Hackneys which he stabled at his 5,000 acre Shelburne Stud on the shores of Vermont's Lake Champlain, and he set out trying to upgrade the standard of locally bred horses using his recent imports. In 1891 he purchased Matchless of Londesboro' from Henry Fairfax. Unfortunately, he received little support from the farmers. In Vermont there were already American trotters and Morgan horses, and the locals, who were very traditional in their outlook, were not prepared to try something new when what they had already met their needs very adequately. Seven years later 100 of Dr Webb's Hackneys were auctioned off at the American Horse Exchange in New York, where the high prices they made reflected the demand for Hackneys among more progressive American buyers.

One of the great pioneers of the Hackney in America was John A. Logan, Jnr, proprietor of the Oriole Stud in Ohio where a number of fine imported stallions stood at stud including Bonfire, a 15.2 hand chestnut with white legs bred by John Franks of Bridlington and described as 'a perfect Yorkshire Hackney type'; Young Derby, a

Mr and Mrs W. B. Watkins of Virginia, U.S.A., driving their pair of Hackney geldings on a driving club rally. (*Photo: Lucy Brown*)

Yorkshire-bred son of Lord Derby II; Lord Rufus, a chestnut bred by J. N. Anthony of King's Lynn; and Warrior, a bay horse bred by John Young of Garton Grange in Yorkshire. Logan did much to market the Hackney to fellow Americans, and on 5 May 1892 even organised an open day and horse show on his 1300-acre stud to which he invited local society and equestrian people who, according to a writer in *Frank Leslie's Weekly*, 'surrounded the exhibition ring seated in their fashionable equipages'. The show comprised stallions, mares and foals, and youngstock as well as harnessed Hackneys, including three driven pairs and two four-in-hands. An official programme presented to guests gave details of each Hackney shown, and the event was reviewed by *Turf, Field and Farm* magazine who said of the horses: 'It is doubtful if a more valuable or better collection has ever been imported to America.'

The showing of Hackneys in America did not really take off until the second decade of the twentieth century when wealthy exhibitors like 'Judge' W. H. Moore began importing and breeding horses especially for the showring. The Hackney had great appeal for the American showmen who loved flashy horses with extravagant action, and the shows at Madison Square Garden and elsewhere soon boasted large classes of good horses, many of which were English imports. Since then, Hackney studs have been set up in many parts of North America and, unlike the Argentinians who were interested in horses only, the Hackney pony also found many enthusiasts in both the United States and Canada. As early as 1891 the National Horse Show included a class for Hackney ponies and from the many excellent ponies imported in the early years of the breed, including Berkeley Bantam for whom 'Judge' Moore paid £1,600 in 1904, some of the top studs were formed, such as Macy Willets' Cassilis Stud in Massachusetts where many champions were bred.

Among the many notable British-bred ponies imported over the years, one pony of special significance was King of the Plain, bred by Arthur Humphrey of Morton, near Gainsborough, in whose ownership he won the class for two-year-old colts at the 1927 Hackney Horse Society show at Doncaster. Purchased by Bertram Mills later that year on behalf of Mr J. R. Thompson of Chicago, the record-priced pony won the championship stakes at Toronto and Chicago the following season and continued to be a prolific winner in the showring for some years to come. As a breeding stallion, King of the Plain, who was a great-grandson of the famous stallion Sir Horace, was no less successful and he produced a string of prizewinning ponies, including Highland Cora, believed by many to have been one of the best harness ponies of all time. On two occasions during her lifetime, she changed hands for the high price of $15,000. While King of the Plain was a great asset to American Hackney pony studs, his move across the Atlantic was a real loss to British breeders. However, in 1993, Neville Dent, chairman of the Hackney Horse Society, imported two American-bred descendants of King of the Plain, a yearling colt and a two-year-old filly, both by Dufferin Tycoon, which he regards as a gene bank for future Hackney pony breeding programmes.

Apart from the Hackney's role in the development of the Standardbred trotter, some people also believe that Justin Morgan, foundation sire of the Morgan breed, was a Norfolk Roadster. Alexander Cassatt, writing in 1892, said that 'Bellfounder is believed to have had much to do with the creation of the Morgan family', while John A. Logan went further and declared that 'the Morgan breed is almost pure Hackney', although both claims are impossible to substantiate. Hackney horse stallions were used in the development of the American Saddlebred, and Hackney pony blood was occasionally and discreetly employed in 'improving' the Welsh and Shetland breeds in America.

When Count Alexis Grigorievich Orlov, a Russian nobleman and owner of vast estates at one time employing 30,000 serfs, produced in the 1770s the breed of trotting horse which now bears his name, he used foundation stock of many breeds and types. At his Kraenovai Stud he had twenty-two English-bred stallions and fifty-three English-bred mares, and although the majority were Thoroughbred there is reason to believe there may have been Yorkshire Trotters among them for the Count was especially interested in trotting horses. Among the Thoroughbreds which influenced the early Hackneys in Yorkshire was a stallion called Regulus, and a grandson of this horse named Tandem was one of the breeding stallions listed at the Count's stud.

In its home country, the Hackney was used in the development of several native pony breeds including the Welsh Cob, which in its early years was renowned like the Hackney as a fast and tireless trotter. The cobs were bred up from Welsh Mountain pony mares by the addition of outside blood, and in an article on Montgomeryshire horses, written in 1900, the author, a Mr Halford, looking back over the preceding sixty years, stated: 'size has been obtained by crossing with larger sires, principally with more of the Yorkshire than of Norfolk blood'. Welsh cattle drovers who made regular trips to the east coast were responsible for introducing the Hackney blood into Wales, either by bringing stallions home with them or by getting the native Welsh mares they were mounted on covered by Hackney stallions while they were in the eastern counties. As Halford said, the Hackney he remembered 'had good shoulders and rode well', but he added: 'of late years – and I think partly owing to the formation of the Hackney Society – a different class of Hackney has been located near Welshpool'. These later imports were more of a harness type with more action, and their progeny were described by Halford as 'cobs more suited for harness than for saddle'. Four Hackney stallions, one pure-bred, three part-bred, had particular influence on the Welsh Cob. Alonzo The Brave, foaled in 1866, a bay horse standing 15.3 hands and a direct descendant of Old Shales, was the only pure-bred Hackney; True Briton, bred in Clydogau, Wales in 1830 by John Walters, was out of an Arab mare by a Yorkshire Coach Horse; Trotting Comet, a 15.2 hand horse, foaled in 1836 and 'famous throughout Wales as a sire' was by Flyer, a well-known trotting horse; and Cymro Lloyd, a dun, was said to be by an imported Arab out of a trotting mare. All four were registered in the Hackney stud book, and for many years Welsh Cobs were registered in the same stud book, thus indicating the links between the two breeds at the time. Around 1905, David Evans, a noted Welsh breeder, reported that 'cobs by registered Hackney stallions out of little Welsh ponies and cob mares have lately been selling for up to 500 guineas', and the Hackney/Welsh Cob cross was once so favoured by tradesmen in the capital for delivery work that they were nicknamed 'London cobs'. This cross is still very popular today for harness work, particularly driving trials. The style of showing Welsh Cobs today bears many similarities to the way in which Hackneys are exhibited, and at the Royal Welsh Show at Builth Wells cob stallions are still shown in show wagons and viceroys in the harness classes.

The Norfolk-bred Hackney pony stallion, Pick Up, winner at the 1886 and 1888 Hackney shows and described as 'the beau ideal of a cob stallion', ended his days in Hampshire where he was sent to breed on to New Forest pony mares, and Hackney blood was not infrequently slipped into the Fell breed too. At their meeting in 1916, the Fell Pony Committee for Cumberland, Westmorland and North Yorkshire agreed that crossing with Hackney ponies of the Wilson type should be discouraged as the latter 'had too much Hackney character for local needs'.

Towards the end of the last century, Anthony Hamond, who chaired the first meeting of the Hackney Stud Book Society, sent a 14.2 hand Hackney stallion called Bluebeard up to Sir Samuel Scott's estate in Scotland where he was bred on to Highland pony mares. The secretary of the Hackney Society, Henry Euren, was sufficiently impressed with the good results of this cross that other Scottish breeders including Alexander Morton were persuaded to emulate the example and use Hackneys on hill pony mares. In a report to the Highland and Agricultural Society of Scotland in 1896, Euren assured breeders that Alexander Morton had 'sold the produce of a Hackney stallion and a Scotch pony mare for as much as 200 guineas', and he urged breeders to consider Hackneys 'should they resolve on breeding up the hill stock of the Highlands and Islands'. There is no evidence of the Highland pony being directly influenced by the Hackney as these cross-breds were either sold as working animals or bred back to the Hackney again. George Robb, manager of the Caledonian Railway Company, told Euren that the part-bred progeny of a roan Hackney stallion introduced into the Aberdeen district some years earlier were used by the Company for the lighter work of carriers with great success.

The Dartmoor pony received a shot of Hackney pony blood in the latter part of the last century when a breeder on the moor ran a brown stallion by Christopher Wilson's famous pony, Sir George, with selected Dartmoor mares. Following an in-breeding programme similar to that pursued by Wilson, only the best of the resulting progeny were retained to be in-bred again but, although the experiment was successful, it had little impact on the breed as the excellent prices the stock made ensured that they were sold off the moor rather than absorbed into the general breeding stock.

Some experimental work using Hackneys to upgrade pony stock was conducted in Ireland under the direction of the Congested Districts Board, one of whose chief advisers was Sir Walter Gilbey, and the Board bought forty-one Hackney stallions in total and distributed them around the counties. Eighteen of these Hackneys found their way into the Connemara area, home of Ireland's only native pony breed, but reaction to their influence appears to have been mixed. One speaker, Major Ruttledge-Fair, giving evidence to the Horse Breeding Commission, said that 'the introduction of Hackney sires has been generally appreciated by the people', but other speakers were more critical. Harry M. Donnell said that 'the Hackney is condemned by the outer people altogether, they won't touch him', while Samuel Johnson said he felt 'the use of Hackney sires would soften the blood' of native ponies. Yet another contributor, Mr Robinson, reported that he had seen Hackney progeny and did not care for them. The most successful of the imported Hackneys purchased by the Board was Lord Go Bang II, a son of Lord Derby II, bred by George Hart of Hull and foaled in 1882. He was travelled around the districts in the traditional manner, beginning in Letterfrack in 1892 and finishing in Belmullet, Co. Mayo, in 1903 when he was twenty-one years of age, and there is evidence that he was extensively used. When the Connemara Pony Society was formed under the auspices of the County Galway Committee of Agriculture, only those animals of true Connemara type were selected as breeding stock, and the part-bred Hackneys were culled out. During the open discussion at the Society's inaugural meeting on 15 December 1923 at Oughterard, there was disagreement as to the value of using Welsh Cobs, but 'the Hackney blood was discounted and called a failure'.

Whatever its influence on recognised pure breeds of horses and ponies, the impact of the Hackney on types of horses including artillery, pack, draught, carriage, delivery and even farm horses across the world cannot be underestimated. Alexander Morton, one of the leading Hackney breeders in Scotland, said in an address to the Glasgow Agricultural Discussion Society in 1891 that 'there is now scarcely a country under the sun but more or less imports Hackney stallions for breeding purposes', and in most cases this was for the improvement and upgrading of the local stock.

7 High-stepping action: the training of the Hackney

The one characteristic which above all other distinguishes the Hackney from other breeds is its distinctive high-stepping action. But this did not become a feature of the breed until the second half of the nineteenth century, when the demand for stylish carriage horses and the first interest in the Hackney as a show horse instigated the change. Until then the low, ground-covering and fast roadster-type of action had been favoured, but for fashionable carriage work speed was not required as 'a gentleman was never in a hurry', and horses which moved with a slower, loftier cadence began to command the highest prices. The big London horse auctioneers like Tattersalls held weekly sales of carriage horses, the average price of which rose from around £25–£30 in the 1850s to over £1,000 for a well-matched pair by the end of the century. The astute city dealers were continually on the lookout for classy carriage horses for their wealthier and more fashion-conscious customers. 'High action in a carriage horse', wrote the Earl of Onslow in 1889, 'induces the dealer to ask a high price for it', adding that such horses were often seen in the West End of London. They were also regularly driven to elegant carriages in Hyde Park during the 'London season', and many society gentlemen cut a dash on Rotten Row mounted on a high-stepping Hackney. The widening rift between the 'modern' Hackney and the roadster was summed up by an American writer, who perceptively noted: 'the extreme high action which calls forth rounds of applause at the horse show, and is so much admired in the park is not common, nor is it, perhaps, desirable in the roadster'. Not only was the term 'roadster' slipping from common use, the type of horse it described was disappearing along with it.

Although breeding and youngstock classes for Hackneys had been included in the schedules of agricultural society shows for many years, it was not until the 1860s that classes for ridden or driven horses were first staged by some of the more progressive shows. Samuel Sidney, on becoming manager of the London Horse Show in 1864, was largely responsible for these innovative classes, as he felt that the tradition of showing all horses in hand was outdated, and that hunters should be shown under saddle, and carriage horses in harness. His idea met with much interest and, despite the confines of the small arena at the London show, the new ridden and driven classes were popular with exhibitors and spectators alike. Schedule classifications like

'Best phaeton horse' or 'Best gentleman's hack' were aimed at horses with a degree of action, whether shown in harness or under saddle, and the term 'park action' – first used in the London Horse Show's 1868 schedule – came specifically to mean high stepping. At the 1872 show held at the Agricultural Hall in Islington there was a class for 'Park cobs, high steppers' which drew an entry of twenty-one horses.

High-stepping action is a subject which has aroused considerable controversy since it was first introduced for it involves far more than merely raising the feet as high as possible, as differing and subjective opinions will testify. Alexander Cassatt believed that:

> While the knee should be well lifted and nicely rounded, the leg should be thrown well forward from the shoulder; and in the same way behind, the hock cannot be too much bent if the leg receives the proper forward send from the stifle. This is essential, and of the two the action behind is the more important. The delivery should be perfectly straight and true, and the recovery should be quick and snappy.

Up and down 'fighting action' which looks spectacular but covers little ground is incorrect, for the true action of a Hackney must be progressive, and there should be no suggestion of all the action being at the front while the back legs shuffle along. Faulty action like dishing or brushing should be avoided.

The specialised training of Hackneys to achieve high action really began with a man called John Robinson, who was born in Crowle in Lincolnshire in the 1840s. The family moved to County Durham when Robinson was a young boy, and his father, a Scotsman, found employment as a cork maker although he supplemented his income with part-time horse dealing. He was helped in this by his son who often accompanied him to horse sales and fairs where they bought suitable animals, and young John was responsible for breaking the horses as he was a skilful and accomplished rider. When, at the age of nineteen, John married Isobel Burnside, a local girl, he began dealing in his own right, and his early success was in no small way due to his young wife who, as well as being a good horsewoman herself, was more business-minded than her husband. Scouring local horse sales, he purchased any inexpensive animals showing potential, one of which was a young blind pony which he named Gypsy Jack and subsequently taught to high step in the most spectacular fashion. The pony caused a sensation throughout the region and quickly made Robinson's reputation, as well as earning him the nickname of Gypsy Jack, which to his great irritation stuck with him for the rest of his days. The training of another purchase, a black mare named Gypsy Queen, to high step in an equally exaggerated way reinforced Robinson's renown as a horseman, and the sale of the two ponies raised sufficient capital for the Robinsons to extend their horse-dealing activities considerably. They began attending all the well-known horse fairs, buying and selling stepping horses. They travelled from venue to venue by road with Robinson riding one horse and leading a string of up to six others tied head to tail, while Isobel followed behind with their scant luggage in a gig. At the horse fairs and sales, Robinson's competitive nature compelled him to take up any challenges in trotting matches or even flat races in which he always rode bareback, and his numerous wins both lined his pockets and enhanced his reputation.

By the late 1860s, the Robinsons had taken a house with stabling near Beverley in Yorkshire, later moving to Hull where they eventually acquired their own premises. By this time Robinson had become a popular competitor at many of the major shows, winning the class for the best roadster at the 1877 Great Yorkshire Show at York with a mare called Brownbells and repeating his win two years later with a horse called Lady Silvertail when the show was held at Leeds. Over the next twenty-five years, Robinson was to become one of the most successful exhibitors in Hackney and harness classes, either showing his own horses or those of local breeders who engaged his services. He competed at the first show of the Hackney Stud Book Society in 1885 when he showed Princess, a dark chestnut daughter of Lord Derby II, and his famous driving pair of black mares, Lady Julia and Lady Shrewsbury, although as there was no harness classes at the show all three were shown in the in-hand class for mares over fifteen hands. Princess was second behind the show champion, Moore's Princess, and the other two were fourth and fifth respectively in the class of twenty entries. At the 1886 show, Princess was again second in her class while Robinson won the under fifteen hands mare class with a new horse, Apology, whose action, according to Vero Shaw, a ringside spectator, 'was as nearly perfect as possible'. The following year after she had won the championship, Baron de Rothschild paid 1,000 guineas for her. Other big prize winners included the harness pair, Wheel of Fortune and Lady Sykes, sold to the Earl of Shrewsbury for the astronomical sum of £2,000, and Plaisanterie, sold to the American Hackney enthusiast, Alexander Cassatt, and shown for him by Robinson at the Madison Square Garden Show in 1891 where she won her class.

Robinson's most famous horse, however, was the black Hackney gelding, Mornington Cannon, foaled in 1893 and brought out under saddle as a five year old to compete in gentleman's hack classes. Not only had he been taught to trot with the phenomenal knee and hock action which characterised all Robinson's horses, but he cantered like a lady's hack, and over a career which spanned twelve years he won 565 first prizes and forty challenge cups and trophies. Although Robinson owned and trained a large number of successful show horses, Mornington Cannon appeared to be his favourite and he kept the old horse until the end. As an old man living in somewhat reduced circumstances with his grandson in Bridlington, where he died in 1921, Robinson still attended horse sales and shows where he sold framed prints of his famous horses to raise much needed cash.

Robinson's success as a Hackney trainer was largely due to his intuitive understanding of the horses he trained. His grandson, in a eulogy which appeared in the local newspaper following his death, said: 'My grandfather had a marvellous control over horses, and we have known him completely to alter the temper of some vicious animals which came into his hands. He loved as well as understood horses, and it was his love coupled with his instinctive knowledge which enabled him to do what he did.' Although he was by nature a hot-tempered man, he showed infinite patience with his young horses, and J. Fairfax-Blakeborough, who had first-hand experience of seeing Robinson train horses, wrote in his book, *Sporting Days and Sporting Stories*, that Robinson had 'almost more than human control over the horses he showed. He used to say that he could train horses to understand his word of command in the showring much better than he could train men to show them. Many will remember how he used to talk to his horses.' He would spend hours with a horse in long reins to teach it the manners for which his horses were noted, as he knew, in the words of Fairfax-Blakeborough, 'that manners come with long and careful training', and he was aware that without this groundwork to balance his horses and instil basic obedience further training would be ineffective.

When it came to improving the natural action of a horse, Robinson began by getting his young horses physically fit with a regime of riding them out on roads interspersed with working them on recently ploughed ground, preferably heavy clay soil, which helped to muscle them up while encouraging them to lift their feet. Later, the young horses were ridden or driven in long reins over 'bottles', long sheaves of straw mechanically bound by a machine not unlike a binder to form cylindrical rolls with the density and strength of present-day straw bales. These bottles were laid out in rows with the distances in between very carefully measured in relation to the natural length of stride of the horse, which was then trotted over them at a controlled pace. After a short lesson over the bottles, the young horse was walked out on the road. Older horses progressed to work over heavy wooden railway sleepers or wooden beams laid out with the same meticulous attention to distances in between, the purpose of the exercise being to teach the horse cadence and rhythm.

Robinson undoubtedly used other secret training techniques too but if he did he took them with him to his grave. It is likely, however, that he used pastern or fetlock weights in his training programmes and, although they are generally assumed to be a comparatively recent invention, there is evidence to suggest they had been used to obtain more animated action in riding horses since Roman times. Richard Berenger, writing in 1771, describes how the Romans tied rollers of wood on the pastern joints to compel horses to lift their feet so they were 'sufficiently high-stepping for desired elegance of form'. William Browne, who described himself as 'an old northern man' born around 1554, wrote a book entitled *Browne, His Fiftie Yeares Practice*, published in 1624, in which he set down his life's experience in terms of how to train horses 'till they be perfit both for the trot and amble'. The book includes advice on how to develop a 'loftie trot' by the use of wooden spheres of around six inches in diameter which were tied to the pasterns in such a way that they fit in the hollow between the fetlock and the heel. By the nineteenth century, most trainers who used pastern weights had progressed to employing canvas or soft leather sleeves which could be filled with lead shot and tied or buckled around the pastern or lower part of the cannon bone, although others preferred the use of solid lead weights which were strapped or even screwed to the hoof. By the 1890s hardwood rattlers, comprising wooden beads of graduated size threaded on to a fine leather strap and fastened above or below the fetlock sufficiently loosely so that the beads rattle against each other when the animal moves, had made their appearance. In his book, *Die Bearbeitung des*

Hardwood rattlers, used to develop the action of Hackneys. (*Photo: C. Richardson*)

Reit- und Kutschpferdes (*Training of the Riding and Driving Horse*), published in 1896, B. H. von Holleneuffer, an instructor at the Royal Prussian Military Riding Academy in Hanover, describes the use of a simple six-ball rattler. 'The weight and the rattling which occurs as soon as the horse moves', he wrote, 'will encourage the horse to step out more lively and actively.' Extra weight can be achieved by the use of lignum vitae beads, and heavy chain rattlers are occasionally used, although they are generally deemed to be less effective than the more traditional hardwood variety. Rattlers, or anklets as they are sometimes called, need to be employed judiciously for to overweight an animal before it has the necessary muscle power can do untold harm. As one Hackney trainer advised, 'the eye of the master judges the weight'.

The most obvious way to weight the hoof or pastern to improve action is by heavier shoeing and, although this is not effective in all horses, it is beneficial to many. However, any tendency towards faulty or untrue action can be accentuated by the use of heavier shoes, although a good remedial blacksmith may be able to alleviate the problem, and heavier shoes can reduce the length of stride even if the amount of knee and hock flexion is improved. At one time exhibitors were weighting each shoe with as much as three or four pounds of extra metal, and show organisers began imposing maximum weights for shoes in an attempt to regulate the trend. The Hackney Horse Society now has a ruling limiting the weight of shoes used on both horses and ponies at its shows.

Many exhibitors, especially in America, let the front hooves grow very long in the belief that this improves action and, while this can be true within reason, extremely long toes, like over-weighted shoes, can in the long term be detrimental in effect. Francis M. Ware in his book, *Driving* (1903), remarked: 'Shoeing, the weight of the shoes and the appropriate length of the toes have much to do with developing high action', but added that it had become 'the fad to wear the front shoes abnormally and most harmfully long, and not a few horses have been crippled by the practice'.

Some exhibitors resorted to quite bizarre training methods to induce their poor horses to step higher, including working their charges over beds of prickly furze, lungeing them in shallow water or snow, trotting them over rows of carefully spaced ditches, and even cruelly blistering the pasterns before working the unfortunate horse wearing chain rattlers. Some ruthless exhibitors with little regard for their animals even adopted a viciously cruel practice known as cording, whereby a piece of whipcord was tied around the horse's tongue with the ends knotted to the cheekpieces of the bit. When the leadrope was jerked, the severe pain caused to the tongue induced the poor horse to step higher. The practice was banned by the Hackney Horse Society and thankfully disappeared from the showring.

Others employed patent action-improving devices, some of which were quite effective. The most basic design employed felt-lined or padded leather straps which buckled around either the pasterns or fetlocks and from which elasticated cords ran to the girth, shafts of the training vehicle, or elsewhere so that the hoofs were jerked upwards as soon as they left the ground. A variation for use on the front legs only was patented by Thomas Nagle and this had a small pulley hanging from the girth through which a rolled leather strap ran, the ends of which were buckled to fetlock boots so that as one front hoof touched the ground, the other front hoof was pulled right up. Gibsons, the London saddlers, produced their patent action improver in the 1890s and this consisted of the statutory boots on all four lower legs and four independent elasticated straps, the front ones being attached to a ring at the front of a heavy neckstrap not unlike a full horse collar, and the back ones leading to a ring sewn on to the girth of a roller. The apparatus enjoyed considerable commercial success and was used, although rarely admitted to, by many of the top Hackney exhibitors of the day. Even more successful was the system invented by a young Canadian horse tamer called Professor Norton B. Smith who, following in the footsteps of the great American tamer, J. S. Rarey, came to London in 1892 and created something of a minor sensation with a public demonstration of his skills at the Crystal Palace in London. The *Morning Advertiser* described the event as 'a capital show, and well worth a visit', and *The World* newspaper reported that the professor exercised 'a marvellous power over the horses entrusted to him'. He did so with the aid of a simple device he called his double safety rope which gave him considerable control over the difficult horses he dealt with. It consisted of a rope of around twenty feet in length, one end of which was tied securely to a leather strap or boot on the nearside front pastern. The rope was then passed through a large ring on the underside of the pad or roller, down through a ring on the offside front pastern boot, back through the ring on the roller and then to the trainer's hand. Although designed to restrain unruly horses, it also tended to make horses step in an exaggerated fashion, and this did not pass unnoticed by a spectator at one of Smith's popular demonstrations, Robert Black, one of the foremost Hackney trainers of his day. The double safety rope was soon adopted as a training aid by many of the Hackney exhibitors, and variations of it are still used today.

Not everyone approved of these artificial practices to improve action, and Francis M. Ware believed that:

> lunging horses over deep straw beds, through snow or water knee-deep or less, over rails laid at certain distances apart on the ground, using elastic action con-

trollers to knees and hocks when in harness, assisted by proper balancing, will temporarily help action if the horse is allowed to trot only under such circumstances and walked at all other times.

He concluded ruefully that the improvement was rarely worth the trouble. Another critic of artificial devices was the great Hackney enthusiast, Geoffrey D. S. Bennett, who commented that the use of shackles and developers to increase action was harmful to the Hackney breed as it produced a temporary effect on animals with little natural action.

Some training methods produced distinctive types of action like that demonstrated by Menella, the champion mare at the 1906 Hackney Show, who would snatch up her hind legs, hold them for a second and then move them forwards and down without any loss of balance. Sarcastic bystanders referred to her extraordinary hind action as the 'Scotch jerk' but it was to be seen again in other horses trained in the same way. When Menella was bought by the American exhibitor, Judge Moore, her style of training evidently changed for from then on she moved in a more traditional way without the jerking rear action.

Although training can do much to develop and refine action, the essence of good action must come from breeding and be inherent in a young horse before its training begins. The level of natural action in an untrained horse is generally, but not always, an indication of what may be achievable with skilful training. Time and again, trainers will say that action developers or 'boots' as they are generally called will not improve action but they will improve rhythm, timing and cadence. It is said that one of Gypsy Jack Robinson's greatest assets as a producer of high-stepping Hackneys was his ability to recognise potential in young horses, and successful Hackney trainers of later times have evidently shared this intangible talent. Some stallions produce youngstock which show more action naturally than the progeny of other stallions, and others pass on action of a specific type, like the forceful lofty front action for which Polonius' get were noted, or the 'extravagant action and its too frequent deterioration of propelling power' noted in D'Oyley's Confidence's stock. The most successful trainers are able to assess the scope of their pupils and adapt their training methods to suit the individual needs of different horses. Most would probably agree that careful mouthing and initial training are the foundation of developing action, as a well-balanced animal has a tendency to lift its feet more naturally, and if the centre of balance of the horse can be moved further back to make the animal lighter in front the potential to step higher is appreciably increased. As many Hackneys are also highly couraged and keen, careful schooling is important to control their bursting

A Hackney pony foal at the Hurstwood Stud shows its natural action. (*Photo: Bob Langrish*)

energy and channel it into their action. Exhibitors sometimes purposely excite the natural courage of a horse for show wagon classes where an exuberant performance is required, but for private driving classes where perfect manners and less flamboyance are needed a different style of training and presentation in the ring is generally appropriate. Patience in training must also be exercised, for if pressed too soon the young horse will be unable to sustain its action due to immaturity and lack of strength. Correct handling from an early age is advocated by all Hackney exhibitors.

High action did not impress everyone, however, and the Earl of Onslow, writing in the Badminton Library's *Driving* (1889), pointed out that it was a mistake to suppose that there was any advantage in it. 'In the first place', he wrote, 'the horse loses time in lifting his feet up into the air and consequently gets over less ground. Secondly, the concussion which his feet suffer every time he brings them down on the road cannot fail to prove detrimental to their soundness.' He added, 'a horse which steps moderately . . . is likely to prove the most useful and last the longest'. Fourteen years later when the popularity of the Hackney as a show horse had burgeoned and the training of high steppers had become something of an art, Francis M. Ware wrote critically of the 'fancy for extravagant and useless action', and he protested:

93

Contortionists and acrobats of all sizes (and shapes!) have been upheld as marvels provided they can hurl their knees and forefeet to extraordinary altitudes; can snatch their hocks with the abruptness and awkwardness of the victim to stringhalt; and can tear round the ring at a pace impossible and unlawful to pursue in park or on road.

Just as the Hackney altered both in type and in action over the years, the style in which it was shown also changed radically. The accepted way of showing Hackneys at the London Horse Show and elsewhere in the 1860s was for the horses to be led round the ring at a sedate walk by gentlemen in frock coats and top hats, but when classes for horses in harness and under saddle were introduced judges began placing more emphasis on movement and way of going. In harness, the horses were shown in gigs or phaetons, a spider phaeton being particularly favoured, and they were driven at a steady 'park pace' which showed their graceful poised action off to best advantage. Under saddle, they were generally shown in classes for park hacks. S. Sidney in his *Book of the Horse* defined a park hack as 'essentially an ornamental animal . . . he may be an extraordinary weightcarrier, strong as an elephant; but to deserve the prefix of "park" he must have style, if not elegance'. When classes for park hacks were first included in the schedule of the London Horse Show, Henry Frisby, a wealthy stockbroker, entered one of his Hackneys in both the harness class and the saddle class, winning both, and instigating a trend for park hacks which could produce both a stylish high-stepping trot and a smooth, well-balanced canter. Having been developed as a trotting breed, some Hackneys found cantering an awkward pace but those trained for the job like Jack Robinson's Mornington Cannon excelled in this new type of class.

Alexander Cassatt wrote:

> The canter is more or less an artificial pace and need not be referred to in connection with the Hackney except to say that his general conformation, and his way of getting his haunches well under him, make him a very apt pupil in acquiring it, and a very pleasant horse to ride when he has learned it.

Alexander Morton, the Hackney breeder and council member, obviously agreed with him, for in 1891 he said of the Hackney as a saddle horse: 'his response is so sharp, his walk so elastic and full of life, his half-prancing-dancing movements so delightful, that an hour across such an animal affords the keenest enjoyment.'

Another very successful exhibitor of saddle Hackneys was Bill Middleton, the manager of Messrs Baxter's Hutton stud at Brentwood in Essex, who often gave Robinson a run for his money at shows.

In 1897 two classes for ridden Hackneys were included at the Society's London Show and although both attracted good entries they were dropped the following year as the council felt they detracted from the Hackney's main role as a harness breed. Other shows continued to stage saddle horse classes, including the International Horse Show which at its inaugural show at Olympia in 1907 included classes for 'Riding horses, suitable for hacking or park work'. According to the schedule, entrants 'must be practically sound, have good manners, and will be judged as their classification calls for. They will be required to show an even walk, square trot, and free, easy canter. The Judge, or judges will, if necessary, ride those horses they deem worthy to receive awards.' The classes were well supported and the show was a resounding success, thanks largely to the show chairman, Lord Lonsdale, who

Mrs G. Booth's Appleton Blaze, shown by Theresa Shaw in a class for ridden Hackneys, 1990. (*Photo: Jim Moor*)

bedecked the hall with yellow flowers and even brought in his private orchestra to play during the intervals. Classes for ridden Hackneys were revived at the 1913 Hackney show when the classification was split by weight-carrying capacity, one class for horses up to twelve stone, and the other for horses up to fifteen stone, but they were dropped from the schedule the following year. Meanwhile, the park hack classes had veered towards the blood type of horse, and animals with knee and hock action were no longer suitable entrants. However, in the north of England classes for ridden Hackneys continued, although as most were harness horses and not specifically trained as saddle horses they were shown only at a walk and trot. Throughout the 1920s and 1930s many of the larger agricultural shows included classes for Hackneys under saddle, their riders informally attired in baggy 'lion-tamer' breeches, hacking jackets, brown leather leggings and brown boots, and topped with a black bowler hat. The horses were shown in straight-cut saddles and bridles with a curb bit and single rein, and the riders sat well back on their horses' loins with their feet thrust

Ron Castledine riding Mr J. M. Neachell's Heatley Debonair, 1980s. (*Photo: Jim Moor*)

forward in the style of the traditional English hunting seat, which gave the optical illusion of the horse having 'more in front of the saddle' than was often the case. At the trot they leant further back and did not post or rise. The Northern Hackney Show still includes ridden classes, and a press report of the 1989 show at Harrogate noted 'the highlight of the morning being a tremendous class of ten ridden Hackneys, with every rider giving an accomplished performance'. Hackneys are sometimes ridden as part of their training for harness work as this can help towards correct head carriage and collection.

The showing of in-hand horses also underwent a transformation as the sedate top-hatted gentlemen who patronised the early shows were replaced by a new generation of exhibitor whose flamboyant style matched the spectacular action of their charges. 'Trotting sires' conductors', wrote The Druid, 'are generally a set of wild Indians, and show their horses' paces with remarkably jealous zest. They trot them with a long rein, and use words in an almost unknown tongue.' The professional trainers and

Jimmy Davies showing Mr W. T. Barton's famous Hackney stallion, Walton Searchlight, 1958. Post-war exhibitors developed their own style to match the action of the horse. (*Photo: Jim Moor*)

exhibitors who followed in their wake were artists when it came to producing show horses for the ring, and people like Vivian Gooch and the Black brothers set precedents that were difficult to emulate.

The turnout of horses in terms of condition and presentation improved drastically over the years too, although some people including Henry Euren disapproved of the 'over-production' of youngstock at the Hackney shows. 'Year after year at the London Show', he wrote, 'a few young Hackneys have been seen as rough as bears and yet they have won over highly fed animals in the class', as a good judge can assess the merits of a horse without it necessarily being in show condition. Christopher Wilson seemed to share his views when he wrote: 'My Sir George ponies used to lie out all winter, and I only took them up about three weeks before sending them to the Islington Spring Show, where I frequently won with them.' As the quality of animal improved year by year, the standard of presentation rose with it.

Commenting on the styles of showring driving in his foreword to Geoffrey D. S. Bennett's book, *Famous Harness Horses* (1926), Bertram Mills recalled how exhibits were once required to walk around the ring first then trot at a park pace as elegance was aimed for. He added that nowadays they raced into the ring and proceeded to drive faster than they would on the roads. Today, speed is unimportant and present-day styles of showring driving are aimed at encouraging the best performance from individual horses and ponies whose progressive, high-stepping action should be smooth, balanced, free-going and coordinated and, above all, elegant.

Although from the days of the early shows driven Hackneys had traditionally been shown in gigs or stylish four-wheelers, many exhibitors believed that if their horses were put to lighter-weight vehicles the reduced drag factor would permit them to move more freely and show loftier action. Bertram Mills, the professional coachman and founder of Britain's most famous circus, began importing American vehicles around the turn of the century and retailing them through his coachbuilding firm, Mills of Paddington. Through contacts in Ohio and New England, he shipped in large numbers of four-wheeled piano-box buggies including one particular design, the Bailey Wagon, and the vehicles were assembled and finished at his London workshops. These light, hickory-wheeled vehicles became so popular with Hackney exhibitors that there were classes for Hackneys shown in Bailey Wagons at some of the London shows. The great disadvantage of this type of vehicle was that only a limited turning lock could be achieved with the front wheels before they touched the sides of the vehicles, and some had rollers fixed to the body on either side against which the wheels could turn to reduce the risk of the vehicle being damaged or tipping over. In the tight confines of the showring, this lack of manoeuvrability was a

Mr J. H. Chicken's pony, Flashwood Vulcan, driven by Georgina Turner. The vehicle is a viceroy. (*Photo: Jim Moor*)

great disadvantage, so Mills introduced a higher version of the vehicle with an arch cut under the seat to permit the wheels to turn without hindrance. At the time, he was showing a Hackney called Grand Viceroy for Ella Ross, the well-known Manchester exhibitor, and he named his new vehicle a Viceroy in honour of the old horse. Modern show wagons and viceroys are mounted on pneumatic-tyred wire wheels but in all other respects they resemble the light, elegant American-style vehicles with a single seat and patent leather dashboard which Bertram Mills popularised. Both designs of vehicle are really suitable only for single harness use, although most have detachable shafts so that either horse or pony shafts can be fitted. In order to detract as little as possible from the animal between the shafts, these vehicles are invariably painted black with little or no lining, and are exhibited without lamps or other accoutrements, and for the same reason lightweight black harness with a fine breastcollar and false breeching is generally chosen. Bearing reins are standard as their use raises the horse's head in such a way that it encourages more extravagant action, and for this same reason they are sometimes used on stallion tack for showing in hand. A lightweight four wheeler like a spider phaeton is most suitable for Hackney pair classes.

As show wagons and pneumatic-tyred vehicles are debarred from private driving classes, gigs or dogcarts or ralli cars are favoured single harness vehicles, and the

Hackney horse, Manorside John, driven by Con Moran, 1989. Lightweight harness with Tilbury tugs, a breastcollar and false breeching is usual in a show wagon class. (*Photo: Jim Moor*)

100

Mrs Janice Clough driving Grants Tutor in a private driving class. Gig harness with a full collar and breeching is appropriate for this type of class. (*Photo: Jim Moor*)

harness should be more substantial, preferably with a full collar. Lamps should also be carried on the vehicle. For both types of class, gentleman whips should wear a suit, soft leather or dogskin gloves and a bowler hat, although on formal occasions a top hat may be worn, and lady whips should wear a conservatively coloured outfit, gloves and a narrow-brimmed hat. A driving apron or knee rug should be worn, and a whip carried at all times.

8 The Hackney today and in the future

Few breeds are static, and there is rarely, if ever, a point at which any breed is generally agreed to have reached its full potential and stopped developing. Had the Hackney remained the general purpose ride and drive utility horse it was 150 years ago, it would probably not have survived far into the twentieth century, but as a show harness animal it was able to weather the motorised age that ousted other breeds like the Yorkshire Coach Horse, and maintain its popularity up to the present day.

It is a characteristic of the elderly to look back and declare that the things of their youth were better than those of today. This dictum is not infrequently applied to Hackneys, the implication being that the breed has in some way degenerated over the last fifty or more years. Modern examples of the breed are certainly different to their predecessors as the Hackney has continued developing throughout this century, but they are not necessarily inferior as the market whose demands and fashions tend to direct the breed has also changed with the intervening years. When in the 1890s, foreign buyers sought larger, heavier horses, the English breeders obliged by producing a bigger, rangier and more coachy type of Hackney than the smaller and speedier roadster of earlier years. When high-stepping action became popular and the Hackney moved literally into the showring, the old-fashioned type of horse was no longer needed, and breeders concentrated on turning out stylish horses with extravagant action and more quality. An attempt in the 1920s by the Hackney Horse Society to hang on to the old type of Hackney by staging classes at their annual show for stallions suitable for breeding military horses met little success. The motorisation of armies throughout Europe meant that the demand for troop horses was waning, and the exhibits in these classes were viewed with derision by the Hackney showmen who were well aware that the future of the Hackney lay in the showring and not on the battlefield.

Throughout this century, selective breeding of both Hackney horses and ponies has refined the breed and introduced considerably more quality. Some believe that the occasional and judicious use of Thoroughbred blood has contributed to this improvement, but without any loss of breed character as Thoroughbreds figured largely in many of the early Hackney pedigrees so it was essentially a reinforcement of foundation blood rather than an outcross. In-breeding and line breeding to successful show animals has helped establish those qualities most desirable in the showring Hackney, and this has resulted in a slight and gradual shift in the general stamp of animal as there is inevitably a clear link between conformation and the predisposition to high step.

Life-long enthusiasts of the breed who spectated at the Hackney shows of fifty years ago will speak of the substantially built, almost cobby animals frequently shown at the time. While they may have had more bone and greater muscularity than some modern examples of the breed, their closer relationship to the old-fashioned type of road Hackney also meant that many lacked the quality and elegance of action generally associated with today's selectively bred Hackneys.

With the move away from the coach-horse type of Hackney developed for the export trade, there was some reduction in the size of horses, which was welcomed by many of the old Hackney men who maintained that 15.2 hands was the ideal height for the breed. The average size of Hackney ponies has never really altered and although many ponies, especially in the early days, were the under-sized progeny of full-size Hackney horse stallions, their height remained at between twelve and four-teen hands over subsequent generations. Even today, the Hackney Horse Society permits the registration of progeny from Hackney horse/Hackney pony cross parentage.

Although once bred in a wide variety of colours, most present-day Hackneys are bay, brown, chestnut or black, bay being most common, although there is no restriction imposed by the Hackney Horse Society on the colours permitted in animals for registration. Chestnuts are now far less common than they once were, and greys and duns are never seen but there are occasional roans. Some exhibitors favour animals with white markings on all four legs as they feel this emphasises the animal's action, and occasionally examples are shown with sufficient white markings extending up the legs and on to the body to classify the bearers as technically skewbald.

While years of selective breeding have brought many improvements to the breed, one possible casualty is temperament, as many of today's Hackneys have the reputation for being volatile in nature, a trait critics blame on in-breeding but enthusiasts say is essential in a controlled form in a successful show animal. Hackneys have always been highly couraged, and showmen employ this quality in the ring, as a fit horse bursting with energy is likely to produce the sort of exuberant and spectacular performance that people expect in a show wagon class. Few modern-day Hackneys have to work as hard as their predecessors did, and their surplus energy is not infrequently misinterpreted as a gassy and even neurotic nature, but breeders insist that if handled firmly and sympathetically most Hackneys have excellent temperaments.

What is of considerable significance is that the breed standard for the Hackney has never altered since the early years of the Society, nor has there ever been a call to update or amend it, possibly because the Hackney's development over the last hundred years

Miss Pauline Peters driving Mr J. Peters' Brookfield Gold Flake. Some exhibitors believe white socks emphasise a horse's action. (*Photo: Jim Moor*)

has been achieved within the standard of excellence first set down by Alexander Morton back in 1891. The intervening years have seen greater standardisation within the breed, much of the credit for which is due to the work of the Hackney Horse Society, and the modern Hackney horse and pony virtually share the same breed standard.

The body should be compact, and short in the back with well-sprung ribs and plenty of heart room. The shoulders should be well laid back and the quarters strong and broad with well let down hocks and the tail not set too low. A quality head with large bold eyes and small expressive ears, especially in a pony, and set on a neck of medium length with a good top line is desirable, and the legs should be strong and well-formed with large clean joints, plenty of flat bone, and well-shaped feet. The action is paramount, and the trot should be lofty and rounded but ground-covering with no suggestion of dishing, plaiting or other untrue way of going. Correct head carriage can greatly influence how an animal moves, and the way in which a horse has been trained and is driven will also have an important bearing on its movement. The animal should move evenly all round with the hocks well engaged, and the forelegs moving from the shoulder and not the elbow, and the overall picture should be one of rhythm, cadence, poise and elegance. In addition, Hackney ponies must possess indisputable pony character and move in a sharper, snappier manner than their larger, more stately counterparts. A good, bold, long-striding walk is also expected, for as Henry Euren noted 'the walk of a Hackney is quite as noteworthy a characteristic as its trot'.

Although much has been said over the years concerning the concussive effects of high action on a Hackney's legs and hoofs, especially if driven on the hard road, the breed is not prone to unsoundness. In an effort to prove this, the Hackney Horse Society passed a ruling which came into effect at the London Show on 3–6 March 1896 whereby all horses had to pass a veterinary examination prior to coming before the judges. That year 203 out of the 209 stallions examined passed, as did 157 of the 165 mares, and all the 28 geldings, an overall pass rate of 96.5 per cent. Another rule stated that the Society's medals, competed for at shows across the country, could only be issued to animals for which a veterinary certificate of soundness was held, a copy of which had to be sent to the Society's office. By ensuring that soundness was a priority in the breeding stock registered in the early stud books, it became a characteristic of the breed and hereditary unsoundness is still unknown in the Hackney.

The Hackney Horse Society, which celebrated its centenary in 1983, is responsible for recording the registrations of both horses and ponies, which now average about 140 a year, as well as for all other activities which promote the breed. The council has been slightly reduced in size since the Society was originally formed and now comprises twenty-one members, a third of whom stand down each year but are eligible for re-election if nominated, and all recommendations and proposals concerning the Society's work are put before the council for discussion and approval prior to being implemented. The Society has been issuing its own stallion licences since the Ministry of Agriculture transferred responsibility for licensing to individual breed societies in the early 1980s, and all stallions are examined by a veterinary surgeon to ensure they are free from hereditary unsoundness before a licence is issued. The Society also still issues export licences for any registered horses or ponies being sold abroad, and maintains a list of approved judges which is made available to any shows or organisations affiliating to the Society.

In 1994, membership of the Hackney Horse Society stood at around 640, although

Neville Dent, chairman of the Hackney Horse Society, with some of his Hackney pony mares at Harthill Stud, Dorset. (*Photo: Annie Dent*)

if the membership of the Hackney breed societies in other countries is also counted a more accurate figure of the number of Hackney enthusiasts worldwide subscribing to an appropriate society could be collated. There is some liaison between the societies, especially with regard to registrations, and the Hackney Horse Society will accept animals bred and registered abroad if the pedigree of the animal can be confirmed. In the case of animals bred in Canada or Argentina, for example, it is usual to check their breeding back five generations, but with Dutch-bred horses, into which Gelderland blood may have been introduced, the Society may deem it necessary to check the pedigree back further to assure itself of the animal's eligibility for registration in the stud book. In 1993 blood-typing was introduced as mandatory before any animal could be registered with the Hackney Horse Society. This led to a slight reduction in the number of horses and ponies registered that year, although it is expected that registration numbers will increase again over the next few years. A grading system for breeding animals which have bred prize-winning stock and/or are prize winners themselves is now operated by the Society. Breed registration figures for other countries tend to fluctuate a little, although those for the United States have nearly doubled since 1906 when the number stood at 459.

Perhaps the highlight of the Society's year is the annual Hackney Horse Society Show which is held at Ardingly in June, and which represents the culmination of months of planning and preparation for many exhibitors. It is also, most importantly, a shop window through which the Society can market the breed, and every year a number of potential foreign buyers can be found at the ringside. In 1975, Schroder Life, the insurance and financial planning division of merchant bankers, J. Henry Schroder Wagg and Co. Ltd, sponsored the annual show for the first time, and their financial support, which included the prestigious Schroder Life National Hackney Harness Horse and Pony of the Year Championships, continued and developed up until 1992. Schroder Life also generously contributed to breed publication material, which is particularly appropriate as one of the founding members of the Hackney Horse Society council in 1883 was Baron von Schroder who, in 1908, was elected president of the Society.

At the centenary show in 1983, there were entries from Holland and Italy and a special parade of Hackneys organised by Frank Haydon to demonstrate the versatility of the breed in different roles but, unfortunately, H. M. The Queen, who had honoured the Society by becoming president, was unable to attend the show due to the General Election. Lord Margadale, on behalf of the Society, later presented Her Majesty with two plates showing examples of the 1883 and 1983 Hackney horse, and in a message to the Society The Queen expressed her thanks for the plates which were added to her personal collection. While Schroder Life sponsored the harness classes, the breeding classes were sponsored by the Racecourse Betting Levy Board.

As part of the 1983 centenary celebrations, the Hackney Horse Society staged an exhibition of Hackney memorabilia at the annual show at Ardingly which was much admired. Displayed items included medals won at the first Hackney shows, stud cards, photographs, paintings and early prints of famous horses, and part of the material was retained for future displays. In 1992, and with the support of the Borough of Luton, the collection of items was put on permanent display in the first Hackney Horse Society museum at the Stockwood Country Park, near Luton in Bedfordshire, where it is housed in an annexe of the building custom-designed to hold the famous Mossman collection of horsedrawn vehicles.

After the last war when Hackneys started to increase in popularity again, a Northern Hackney Club was started up in the Manchester area as some northern members felt that the breed was not well catered for in the north, particularly in terms of show classes. The Club is now more or less a show society affiliated to the Hackney Horse Society and organises an annual show as well as social functions and an Annual General Meeting.

Hackney horse champion at the 1985 Royal Windsor Horse Show. (*Photo: Bob Langrish*)

In 1993, the first Hackney Horse Society official sale of stock was planned but, sadly, the sale had to be cancelled due to lack of support. As breeders have always managed to sell their Hackneys privately from home, they question the need for an official breed sale. However, such an event would have been convenient for buyers as it would have enabled them to see a selection of animals together in one place at one time, and the general publicity value of a sale is indisputable.

Many of the Hackney societies in other countries also organise their own shows as well as encouraging the inclusion of Hackney classes at the larger national shows. In Canada the important shows are the National Exhibition and the Royal Winter Fair, while the American Hackney Horse Society members, having no breed show of their own, exhibit at shows affiliated to the American Horse Shows Association and offering suitable classes. In-hand or halter classes, as they are described at American shows, tend to be few and far between but harness classes are more popular. Animals are shown at a 'park trot', which is described as being 'executed in a highly collected manner', and, in all but amateur, ladies' or novice classes, at an undefined pace called simply 'show your pony' which permits the exhibitor to select the speed which shows the pony to best advantage. Although Hackney ponies not exceeding 12.2

108

hands are always shown with a long and unbraided mane and tail, larger ponies and horses must according to the rules of the American Horse Shows Association 'appear to have a short tail' as well as a plaited mane. Docking has been illegal in Canada for nearly seventy years and, although it is also illegal in some American states, it is permitted in others. Thus animals are frequently shipped across state boundaries to be docked in order that they comply with show rules without implicating their owners in an illegal practice. Showing styles tend generally to be more theatrical in America than in Britain or on the continent, but the American Horse Shows Association rule book states that Hackney entries 'must be shown without artificial appliances (e.g. wired ears)', adding that 'inconspicuously applied hair in mane or tail, a tail brace and mouth controls are permitted'. Hackney classes at South African, Australian and New Zealand shows are now well established, and in Holland they enjoy tremendous support.

The revival of interest in driving in the 1950s, not as a means of transport but as a leisure activity, gave the Hackney an unexpected opportunity to move out of the showring and again demonstrate its capabilities in other fields of activity. The misconception that the breed was suitable exclusively for exhibiting in show wagon classes was believed by many of the newcomers to pleasure driving, and was to persist like a stigma for some years, but others saw the Hackney as having more scope and, as the popularity of driving increased, Hackneys began appearing in many different roles.

Its greatest impact was in private driving classes which were being reintroduced to the schedules of many agricultural and horse shows. The Hackney was ideal for such classes, as the sort of park driving the breed was adapted for at one point in its history was the type of driving these new classes were based upon. The term 'private driving' restricted entries to owner-driven vehicles, as opposed to either coachman-driven vehicles like Victorias or trade vehicles like butcher's carts, and the judging criteria demand that the horse be of suitable driving type, free moving and well mannered at all times. The harness must also be sound and well fitting, the vehicle roadworthy and of a correct type and size for the horse, and the cleanliness and overall condition of the whole turnout, the appointments like lamps, the dress of the driver or whip, and the performance of the horse are all taken into account. Exaggerated action, like excessive speed, is not required and for this reason Hackneys began to be debarred from many driving classes, particularly as they tended to overshadow less stylish exhibits with their exuberant action and presence. Many of the larger shows now split their private driving class into Hackney and non-Hackney sections, but at other shows the private driving class may flatly debar Hackneys. The training of a

Mrs Wendy Skill driving her Hackney pony in a private driving class in the 1980s. (*Photo: Ken Ettridge*)

Hackney for a private driving class is quite different to that for a show wagon class, and it is frequently argued that if a Hackney adequately meets the criteria by which private driving classes are judged, especially in terms of manners and general paces, it should not be excluded. In American show schedules, private driving classes are usually referred to as pleasure driving classes, but the criteria for judging remain similar.

Concours d'elegance classes are included in the schedules of some of the specialist driving shows and for these the normal rules of judging do not apply. Entrants are judged from a distance by an artist who selects the most elegant turnout. Hackneys are eligible for these classes and are frequently and inevitably among the prize winners.

Tradesmen's turnout classes are another favourite class in which to exhibit Hackneys, as the breed has traditionally been used by all classes of tradesmen, most

Eddie Buck driving his Hackney stallion, Holypark Tarquinius, the winner of a number of *concours d'elegance* classes, including Wembley. (*Photo: Jim Moor*)

Pure and part-bred Hackneys are popular in trade turnout classes. This one is driven to a butcher's box cart. (*Photo: Ken Ettridge*)

especially butchers, who loved a high stepper and also needed a fast horse to use on delivery rounds in the days before refrigeration. An eye-catching horse drew attention to the tradesman's cart and helped attract custom.

One of the main criticisms levelled against the Hackney was that, after years of selective breeding for the showring, it had lost its stamina and powers of endurance. It was believed that Hackneys like County Member Junior, a British-bred grandson of Lord Derby II, who on his expatriation to the USA held the Long Distance Road Championship of America, were things of the past, and that the modern Hackney had no staying power. County Member Junior earned his title on 12 December 1893 when, between the shafts of a top buggy carrying two men, he trotted from Lebanon, Kentucky to Danville and back, a distance of seventy-one miles, in seven hours forty-three minutes, including a forty-minute rest in Danville. The road was reported to be very rough in places and there were long and frequent hills to be negotiated, but the feat was officially timed and full details recorded in the local press. The introduction of a new sport, driving trials, was to provide the Hackney with the opportunity it needed to prove it still had stamina. In 1969, the Fédération Equestre Internationale set out the rules and regulations for the running of these demanding driving competitions which originated on the continent. Although the early events were specifically for four-in-hand teams, the classifications were later extended to include pairs, singles and eventually tandems too. Each full driving trials event comprises three separate phases – dressage, a cross country marathon and obstacle cones – and the individual scores from each section are collated to give an overall result. The dressage phase is in the form of a test, which must be driven from memory, comprising a prescribed number of movements involving changes of pace and direction, and is designed to assess the freedom, regularity and distinction of paces, harmony, impulsion, suppleness and obedience of the horse. The same qualities which make Hackneys very eye-catching in private driving classes can also work to their advantage in a dressage test and, providing the animals are schooled to demonstrate clearly defined paces and collection, their general *joie de vivre* and presence can make them very attractive to watch, and the dressage scores they attain is evidence of this.

The cross country marathon is the heart of a driving trial and it really tests the fitness and stamina of a horse. Briefly, the course is usually divided into five sections, three at a trot and two at a walk, with a 'time allowed' calculated for each section so that penalties are accrued for exceeding the time allowance for a section as well as finishing a section before a minimum time. Natural hazards like steep gradients are included in all but the walk sections, and in addition a number of artificial hazards

The excitement of driving trials. Miss S. Smith (*above*) driving her pair of Hackney ponies on the marathon phase of a driving trial (*Photo: Ken Ettridge*); (*below*) Hackney pony, Bowerbank Thomas, driven by Caroline Glennie, at the 1991 Brighton Driving Trials. (*Photo: Annie Dent*)

Versatility is the name of the Hackney's game as demonstrated on these two pages: Hackney horse, Grants Pendant (*opposite page, top*), driven by Emma Cook, on the marathon phase of a driving trial, 1991; a Hackney pony (*opposite page, below*), also competing in a marathon; and (*above*) the part-bred Hackney, Hart Hill Lady Mildred, competing at the Savernake Park Horse Trials in 1991. She is by National Trust (G.S.B) out of the 1986–7 Hackney Horse Society Show senior champion mare, Sefton Louise. (*Photos: Annie Dent*)

are incorporated into the middle trot section. Despite the expectations of many who believed that Hackneys would expend too much energy in their high action to achieve the rigorous section speeds, those animals which competed regularly proved they could maintain the required pace as well as cope with the varied terrain and negotiate the hazards with more nimbleness and celerity than most people expected.

The final phase of the sport is obstacle driving in which competitors have to drive a course of about twenty pairs of cones, sometimes augmented with multiple obstacles built of elements of show jumps, straw bales or poles, within a time allowed.

Here again Hackneys have shown themselves capable of competing favourably with other breeds.

Perhaps the most important thing driving trials has done is to re-establish the Hackney as a performance breed, and in recent years considerable interest has been shown in part-bred Hackneys not only for competitive driving, where there is a ready market, but in other equestrian disciplines too. Many part-bred Hackneys, and one or two pure-breds, have been notable show jumpers, and several outstanding hunters with Hackney blood in their veins have been bred over the years. Being realistic, the Hackney in its pure-bred form has little future as a riding horse of any description as its action generally makes it uncomfortable to ride, but the part-bred is a different matter entirely. In 1993, the Hackney Horse Society, aware that the cross-bred Hackney had great potential in the equestrian market, as it had 100 years ago, opened a part-bred register in its stud book and even included part-bred classes at the Ardingly Show. With greater emphasis being placed on the registration of horses of all kinds, by opening a part-bred section in its stud book the Society ensures that the breed is credited for its successful part-breds. Although the traditional exhibiting of Hackneys in show wagons will hopefully continue into the future, it represents only a small part of the Hackney's scope and potential and if the breed is to expand its reputation and numbers in years to come it is probable that this will be in the part-bred market and performance field. New types of competitive equestrian sport, like long distance driving, are continually being introduced and there is no reason why the Hackney should not adapt to the requirements of these as it has successfully adapted to changing needs since its early days.

The Hackney is indisputably the finest harness horse in the world. How it may further develop in the future is uncertain, but the immense popularity it now enjoys both with the equestrian fraternity and the general public is likely to be sustained, for high steppers, like heavy horses, have always attracted admiration and interest. With a healthy world population of Hackneys, active breed societies in several countries, and more and more attention being focused on the horse as a part of our leisure activities, the prognosis for the Hackney is reassuring and it will undoubtedly remain one of the world's most distinctive breeds.

Bibliography

Beaufort, Duke of. *Driving* (The Badminton Library), Longman, Green & Co., 1889

Bennett, Geoffrey D. S. *Famous Harness Horses*, Welbecson, 1926

Brocklebank, Sylvia A. *The Road and the Ring*, ed. T. Ryder, Horse Drawn Carriages, 1975

Browne, W. *Browne: His Fiftie Yeares Practice*, John Piper, 1624

Charlton, R. B. *A Lifetime With Ponies*, Abbey Press, 1944

Dent, A. A. *Horses in Shakespeare's England*, J. A. Allen, 1987

Dent, A. A. *Cleveland Bay Horses*, J. A. Allen, 1978

Dent, A. A. and Machin Goodall, D. *A History of British Native Ponies*, J. A. Allen, 1988

Fairfax-Blakeborough, J. *Sporting Days and Sporting Stories*, P. Allen, 1925

Gilbey, Sir W. *The Harness Horse*, Vinton, 1898

Gilbey, Sir W. *Thoroughbred and Other Ponies*, Vinton, 1903

Gilbey, Sir W. *Horse Breeding in England and India and Army Horses Abroad*, Vinton, 1901

Gordon, W. J. *The Horse World of London*, The Religious Tract Society, 1893

Holleneuffer, B. H. von. *Die Bearbeitung des Reit- und Kutschpferdes zwischen den Pilaren*, Hanover, 1896

Lawrence, J. *Philosophical and Practical Treatise on Horses*, T. N. Longman, 1796

Lawrence, J. *The History and Delineation of the Horse*, Albion Press, 1809

Logan, J. A., junr. *The Oriole Stud of Hackneys*, privately published, Ohio, 1892

Lynn, P. *Shrouded in Mist*, privately published, 1984.

Marshall, J. *The Rural Economy of Norfolk*, 1787

Merwin, H. C. *Road, Track and Stable*, Little, Brown, 1892

Miles, W. J. *Modern Practical Farriery, A Complete Guide to all that Relates to the Horse*, McKenzie, 1868

Morgan, N. *Perfection of Horsemanship*, Edward White, 1609

Richardson, Charles. *The New Book of the Horse*, Cassell, 1910–11

Richardson, C. *Driving, The Development and Use of Horse Drawn Vehicles*, Batsford, 1985

Richardson, C. *The Fell Pony*, J. A. Allen, 1990

Righyni, S. I. *Hackney Horses and Hackney Ponies*, Hackney Horse Society, 1948

Ryder, T. *The High Stepper*, J. A. Allen, 1961

Shaw, V. *Guide to the Hackney Horse*, Nimrod Press (reprinted), 1990

Sidney, S. *The Book of the Horse*, Cassell, 1874.

Smith, Norton B. *Practical Treatise on the Breaking and Training of Wild and Vicious Horses*, privately published, London, 1892

Summerhayes, R. S. *The Observer's Book of Horses and Ponies*, Warne & Co., 1949

Taplin, William. *Sporting Dictionary*, Thomas Marden, 1803

de Trafford, Sir Humphrey. *Horses of the British Empire*, Southwood, 1907

Tylden, Major G. *Horses and Saddlery*, J. A. Allen, 1965

Ware, F. M. *Driving*, Doubleday Page, 1903

Wheeling, K. E. *Horse-Drawn Vehicles at the Shelburne Musuem*, Shelburne Museum, 1974

Wilson, J. A. *A Cumbrian Blacksmith*, Dalesman, 1978

Wrangel, Count, *Die Rassen des Pferdes*, Schickhardt & Ebner, 1908

Woodruff, Hiram. *Trotting Horse of America*, Porter & Coates, 1868

Index

Page numbers in italics refer to illustrations.